PAINTED ILLUSIONS

Including Wood-grain, Stone & Metallic Finishes

The Home Decorating Institute®

Copyright © 1996 Cy DeCosse Incorporated 5900 Green Oak Drive Minnetonka, Minnesota 55343
1-800-328-3895 All rights reserved Printed in U.S.A.

Library of Congress Cataloging-in-Publication Data Painted illusions. p. cm. — (Arts & crafts for home decorating)
ISBN 0-86573-402-X (hardcover) — ISBN 0-86573-403-8 (softcover) 1. House painting. 2. Furniture painting. 3. Interior
decoration. I. Home Decorating Institute (Minnetonka, Minn.) II. Cy DeCosse Incorporated. III. Series.   TT323.P33 1996
698'.14 — dc20 96-15853 CIP

CONTENTS

Getting Started

Wood-grain Finishes & More

Marble & Stone Finishes

Metallic Finishes

Trompe l'Oeil Effects

CREATIVE FAUX FINISHES

Images of nature's treasures are creatively transferred to our interiors with faux finishes.

Faux finishes have long been used as artistic solutions to practical decorating problems. For centuries, artists have used painted faux finishes to imitate nature's most precious materials. Where authentic marble has been too costly or too heavy for a building project, faux marble finishes have been painted over less costly, lighter-weight materials. Faux wood-grain finishes have been used to create the illusion of exotic woods, too difficult or expensive to transport across oceans.

Though often a practical option, modern faux finishing also fulfills a desire for self-expression and creativity. For instance, one might paint the illusion of inlaid malachite on drawer fronts, not in an effort to pretend great wealth, but purely for artistic expression. Gold leaf may be applied to a decorative accessory simply for creative enjoyment, rather than to imply that the item is carved from solid gold. Creating the illusion is entertaining for both the artist and the viewer. A stenciled trompe l'oeil image of potted flowers may trick the delighted viewer for only a few seconds, but the satisfaction gained from creating the illusion is renewed with each surprised glance.

Even the amateur faux finisher can create realistic illusions, using easy techniques and specially designed tools. Water-based paints and glazes, used throughout this book, make cleanup easy and are safe for the environment.

All information in this book has been tested; however, because skill levels and conditions vary, the publisher disclaims any liability for unsatisfactory results. Follow the manufacturers' instructions for tools and materials used to complete these projects. The publisher is not responsible for any injury or damage caused by the improper use of tools, materials, or information in this publication.

FAUX FINISHES

The art of faux finishing enables the artist to create painted illusions that tease the viewer into believing they are real. Finishing techniques used with water-based paints and glazes make it possible to imitate wood-grain patterns or create the look of various marbles and stones.

Bird's-eye maple (page 42).

Bone and horn (page 51).

Mahogany *(page 38)*.

Satinwood *(page 40)*.

Burled wood *(page 48)*.

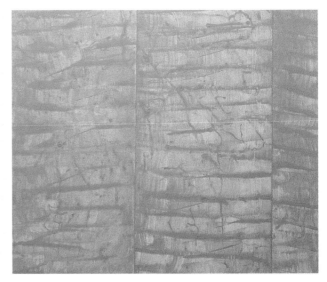

Tiger maple *(page 46)*.

Oak *(page 36)*.

Zebrawood *(page 34)*.

(Continued)

FAUX FINISHES
(CONTINUED)

Tigereye *(page 57)*.

Unpolished stone *(page 84)*.

Malachite (page 64).

Travertine (page 81).

Lapis (page 61).

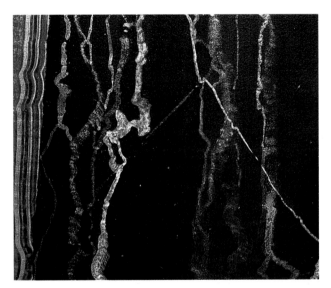

Portoro (page 69).

Serpentine (page 73).

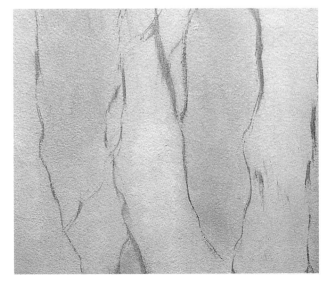

Norwegian rose (page 76).

(Continued)

CREATIVE FAUX FINISHES

FAUX FINISHES
(CONTINUED)

Metallic finishes, including metal leaf and painted finishes, add a touch of elegance to home decorating. Special paints and solutions make it possible to achieve a rich, aged look in minutes.

Antiqued metallic painted finishes (page 96).

Metal-leaf finishes (page 100).

Antiqued metal-leaf finishes (page 105).

Metallic composite stenciling (page 109).

Trompe l'oeil painting creates the illusion of reality by effective use of shading, highlighting, and perspective. These simple trompe l'oeil effects, achieved by either hand painting or stenciling, are not meant to reproduce an image with photographic quality, but rather to tease the viewer into seeing dimension in simplified painted images.

Hand-painted trompe l'oeil *(page 115).*

Stenciled trompe l'oeil *(page 119).*

Combined trompe l'oeil techniques *(page 123).*

Getting Started

WATER-BASED PAINTS & GLAZES

Latex and acrylic paints can be used successfully for a wide range of faux finishes and techniques. Because they are water-based, they are easy to clean up with just soap and water, and they are also safer for the environment than oil-based paints.

Water-based paints also dry quickly, which is not necessarily an advantage in faux finishing, especially for techniques that require some manipulation of the paint on the surface. To increase open time, or the length of time the paint can be manipulated, several paint additives have been developed. These include latex paint conditioner, such as Floetrol®, and acrylic extender.

For some faux finishing techniques, it is preferable to use a paint glaze, which is usually thinner and more translucent than paint. There are some premixed acrylic paint glazes available in limited colors. These may be mixed to acquire additional glaze colors. Untinted acrylic mediums in gloss, satin, or matte finishes are also available for mixing with acrylic or latex paint to make glazes. The glaze medium does not change the color of the paint; generally a small amount of paint is added to glaze medium, just enough to give it the desired color. Latex or acrylic paint can also be mixed with water-based urethane or varnish for a very translucent glaze.

Gloss glaze. Faux finishes, such as marbles and semiprecious stones, have a high gloss that gives them a realistic appearance. Premixed glazes generally dry with a gloss finish. To mix a glaze that will dry with a gloss finish, use acrylic medium that specifies gloss finish, or mix a urethane glaze. Follow instructions on glaze mediums, or mix one part urethane, one part paint, and one part water.

Satin or matte glaze. For a translucent glaze that dries with a satin or matte finish, mix latex or acrylic paint with matte or satin acrylic medium, or mix matte finish acrylic medium into premixed glaze to cut the gloss.

Flat paint glaze. For a faux finish with a naturally flat appearance, such as travertine (page 81) or unpolished stone (page 84), a flat paint glaze can be used. For small surface areas, this may simply mean mixing two parts paint and one part water. For extended open time, desired on a larger surface, use a recipe of one part paint, one part paint conditioner, and one part water. Vary the recipe to suit your own needs.

Wash. A wash is often applied as a final step in a faux finish to add a hint of color tone, or to create depth. A wash is mixed by diluting latex or acrylic paint with water to the consistency of ink. Washes generally have a flat finish.

Low-luster latex enamel paint is used for the base coat under faux finishes. The slightly sheened surface gives the finish a base to cling to, while allowing manipulation tools to move easily on the surface.

Acrylic paints are available in a wide range of colors. They can be used alone for stenciling, or mixed with acrylic mediums to create glazes for faux finishing.

Premixed acrylic paint glazes are available in a variety of colors for faux finishing. They are slightly translucent and contain additives for extended open time.

Acrylic mediums, or glaze mediums, can be mixed with acrylic or latex paint to create paint glazes with gloss, satin, or matte finishes.

PRIMERS & FINISHES

PRIMERS

Most unpainted surfaces must be painted with a primer before the faux finish is applied. The purpose of a primer is to seal the surface and provide a foundation to which the painted finish will adhere well. There are a variety of water-based primers available, each designed to be used on specific surfaces. As with other water-based paint products, these primers dry quickly and brushes or rollers may be cleaned up with soap and water.

Flat latex primer is used for sealing unfinished wallboard. It makes the surface nonporous so fewer coats of paint are needed. This primer may also be used to seal previously painted wallboard before applying new paint of a dramatically different color. The primer prevents the original color from showing through.

Latex enamel undercoat is used for priming most raw woods or woods that have been previously painted or stained. A wood primer closes the pores of the wood, for a smooth surface. It is not used for cedar, redwood, or plywoods that contain water-soluble dyes, because the dyes would bleed through the primer.

Rust-inhibiting latex metal primer helps paint adhere to metal. Once a rust-inhibiting primer is applied, water-based paint may be used on metal without causing the surface to rust.

Polyvinyl acrylic primer, or PVA, is used to seal the porous surface of plaster and unglazed pottery, if a smooth paint finish is desired. To preserve the texture of plaster or unglazed pottery, apply the paint directly to the surface without using a primer.

Stain-killing primer seals stains like crayon, ink, and grease so they will not bleed through the top coat of paint. It is used to seal knotholes and is the recommended primer for cedar, redwood, and plywood with water-soluble dyes. This versatile primer is also used for glossy surfaces like glazed pottery and ceramic, making it unnecessary to sand or degloss the surface.

Gesso is an acrylic polymer emulsion that has been traditionally used to seal artists' canvases. It can also be used very successfully to prime unglazed pottery or plaster, as well as many other surfaces. Because gesso is available in small quantities, it is a more economical choice for small projects than the latex primers.

FINISHES

Transparent finishes can be used over the painted surface to provide protection or to enhance the appearance. For faux marbles and semiprecious stone, the surface looks more realistic if a high-gloss finish is applied. A satin finish gives wood-grained surfaces a genuine appearance. Faux finishes with a naturally flat finish may be left unsealed or, for added protection, may be sealed with a matte finish.

Clear finish, such as water-based urethane or acrylic, may be used over a painted faux finish for added durability. Available in matte, satin, or gloss, clear finish is applied with a brush or sponge applicator. Environmentally safe clear finishes are available in pints, quarts, and gallons (0.5, 0.9, and 3.8 L) at paint supply stores and in 4-oz. and 8-oz. (119 and 237 mL) bottles at craft stores.

Aerosol clear acrylic sealer, available in matte or gloss, may be used as a protective finish over paint. A gloss sealer also adds sheen and depth to the painted finish for a more polished look. Apply aerosol sealer in several light coats rather than one heavy coat, to avoid dripping or puddling. To protect the environment, select an aerosol sealer that does not contain harmful propellants. Use all sealers in a well-ventilated area.

PREPARING THE SURFACE

Careful surface preparation is important for creating beautiful, long-lasting faux finishes. Surfaces must be clean and smooth, and in most cases a primer should be applied to assure that the faux finish will adhere well.

Preparation steps vary depending on the type of material being painted, any previously existing finishes, and the type of finish being applied. Because the finishes in this book use water-based paints and glazes, these preparation steps and suggested primers are designed for that purpose. For example, sanded surfaces are wiped with a damp cloth, rather than a tack cloth, because the oils in a tack cloth may interfere with the adhesion of water-based paints.

Apply primers with foam applicators or low-napped rollers for minimal brush strokes or pebbling of the surface. For finishes that require a smooth, glossy appearance, lightly sand the primed surface with 400-grit wet/dry sandpaper before applying the base coat.

PREPARING SURFACES FOR PAINTING

SURFACE TO BE PAINTED	PREPARATION STEPS	PRIMER
UNFINISHED WOOD	**1.** Sand surface to smooth it. **2.** Wipe with damp cloth to remove grit. **3.** Apply primer.	Latex enamel undercoat.
PREVIOUSLY PAINTED WOOD	**1.** Clean surface to remove any grease and dirt. **2.** Rinse with clear water; allow to dry. **3.** Sand surface to degloss it. **4.** Wipe with damp cloth to remove grit. **5.** Apply primer to any areas of bare wood.	Not necessary, except when touching up areas of bare wood; then use latex enamel undercoat.
PREVIOUSLY VARNISHED WOOD	**1.** Clean surface to remove any grease and dirt. **2.** Rinse with clear water; allow to dry. **3.** Sand surface to degloss it. **4.** Wipe with damp cloth to remove grit. **5.** Apply primer.	Latex enamel undercoat.
UNFINISHED WALLBOARD	**1.** Dust with hand broom, or vacuum with soft brush attachment. **2.** Apply primer.	Flat latex primer.
PREVIOUSLY PAINTED WALLBOARD	**1.** Clean surface to remove any grease and dirt. **2.** Rinse with clear water; allow to dry. **3.** Apply primer, only if making a dramatic color change.	Not necessary, except when painting over dark or strong color; then use polyvinyl acrylic primer.
UNPAINTED PLASTER	**1.** Sand any flat surfaces as necessary. **2.** Dust with hand broom, or vacuum with soft brush attachment.	Polyvinyl acrylic primer.
PREVIOUSLY PAINTED PLASTER	**1.** Clean surface to remove any grease and dirt. **2.** Rinse with clear water; allow to dry. **3.** Fill any cracks with spackling compound. **4.** Sand surface to degloss it.	Not necessary, except when painting over dark or strong color; then use polyvinyl acrylic primer.
UNGLAZED POTTERY	**1.** Dust with brush, or vacuum with soft brush attachment. **2.** Apply primer.	Polyvinyl acrylic primer or gesso.
GLAZED POTTERY, CERAMIC & GLASS	**1.** Clean surface to remove any grease and dirt. **2.** Rinse with clear water; allow to dry. **3.** Apply primer.	Stain-killing primer.
METAL	**1.** Clean surface and remove lacquer, using metal cleaner. **2.** Sand surface to degloss it and remove any rust. **3.** Wipe with damp cloth to remove grit. **4.** Apply primer.	Rust-inhibiting latex metal primer.

TOOLS FOR FAUX FINISHING

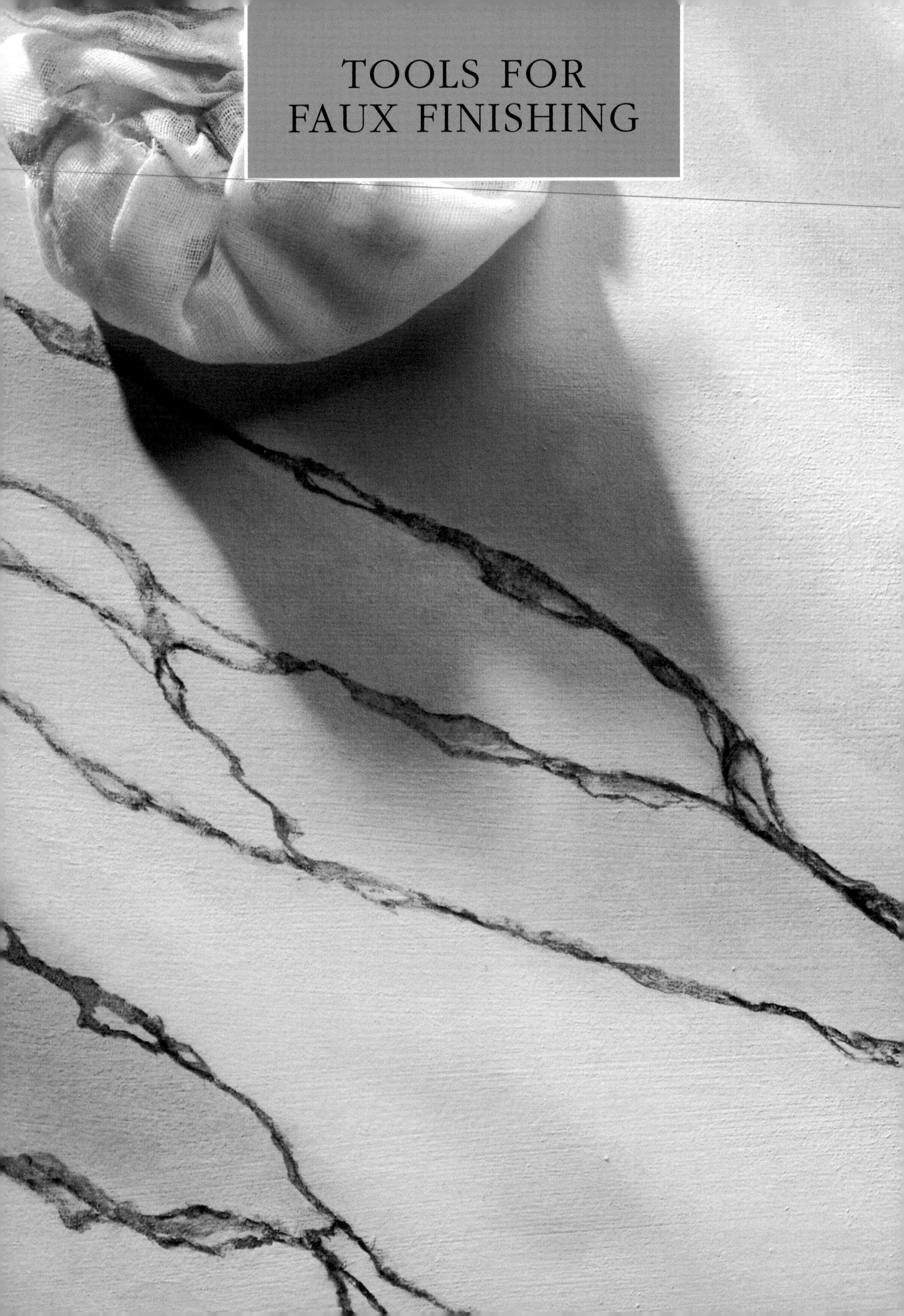

A variety of tools and materials are used in faux finishing. Some tools may have several uses, while others are very specialized. Cheesecloth, for instance, has unlimited use in faux finishing. For best results, purchase prewashed cheesecloth with a tight weave. Many decorative painting tools are common items, such as newspaper, erasers, cotton-tipped swabs, or a toothbrush.

Materials and tools useful for preparing the surface and applying base coats include sandpaper, damp cloth, foam applicators, general-purpose paintbrushes, and rollers. Foam rollers and rollers with ¼" (6 mm) nap are used to apply very smooth base coats. Painter's masking tape and drop cloths are also necessary items to have on hand for masking off and protecting surrounding areas.

Most specialty paintbrushes for faux finishing have natural bristles. Though generally used with oil-based paints, these brushes can also be used successfully with water-based paints. With proper care, natural-bristle brushes will last a long time.

HOW TO CARE FOR NATURAL-BRISTLE PAINTBRUSHES

1 Apply small amount of ordinary hair conditioner to tips of bristles before first use; massage conditioner through bristles. Do not rinse out.

2 Wash brushes used for water-based paints, using mild soap; rinse completely under running water.

3 Reshape bristles, if necessary. Hang brushes by handles to dry, or lay flat. Never allow brushes to dry with bristles pointing up, as this may damage the ferrule. Repeat step 1 when brush is dry.

TOOLS FOR
FAUX FINISHING
(CONTINUED)

d

c

e

f

SYMPHON
8164-5

SYMPHON

b

a

g

Many tools and paintbrushes have been developed for creating specialized faux finishing effects. Depending on how they are used, some tools may create more than one effect. Working with the various tools and learning their capabilities is an important step in becoming a successful faux finisher. Most tools and paintbrushes are available in a range of sizes. As a general rule, use the largest size tool or brush suitable for the surface size.

Some tools and brushes are designed for manipulating the wet glaze on the surface, such as floggers **(a)**, blending brushes or softeners **(b)**, a mottler **(c)**, and stipplers **(d)**.

Certain faux effects are achieved using removal tools, such as a grainer **(e)**, overgrainers **(f)**, wipe-out tools **(g)**, and combs **(h)**. Artist's erasers **(i)** can be notched (page 57) and used as combs.

Specialty brushes designed for applying paints and glazes include artist's brushes, such as rounds **(j)**, liners **(k)**, or a dagger **(l).** These may be used for veining in marble finishes or graining in wood finishes. Stenciling brushes **(m)** are available in ¼" to 1¼" (6 mm to 3.2 cm) diameters. Other tools, such as a sea sponge **(n)** or feathers **(o)** are also used for applying paints and glazes. A check roller **(p)** is a specialty tool used for applying pore structure in a faux oak finish.

GLOSSARY
OF TECHNIQUES

APPLIED TECHNIQUE. Some faux finishes are created by applying glazes to a surface, using specialty tools. Applied techniques are used in many of the marble and stone faux finishes and for developing some characteristics of wood graining, such as heart grain.

BLENDING. Two or more colors of glaze applied to a surface can be mixed together slightly along their adjoining edges, cutting the contrast between them. Blending brushes, also called softeners, have very soft, natural bristles, usually goat or badger hair. This technique is done with a dry brush, very softly sweeping across the surface of the glaze in various directions to lightly coax the colors together and soften any harsh contrasts.

BURNISHING. After masking tape is applies to a surface, whether for creating grout lines (page 88), inlaid designs (page 51), or simply to protect surrounding areas, the edges of the tape are pressed firmly, using the end of a plastic credit card or a thumbnail. This keeps paint from seeping under the tape.

COMBING. Narrow bands or stripes are created as a comb is scraped over a glazed surface, removing some of the wet glaze. Interesting patterns can be produced by combing in various directions and rhythms. Metal and rubber combs, useful in wood graining, are available in a variety of sizes. The edges of a soft artist's eraser can be notched with a razor or mat knife in an irregular pattern to create a comb, as for faux malachite (page 64) and faux tigereye (page 57).

FLOGGING. A dry natural-bristle brush, called a flogger or dragger, is held parallel to the glazed surface and rapidly slapped on the surface in quick, choppy motions, moving vertically from bottom to top. The resulting textured appearance is characteristic of many wood grains. Floggers are thin brushes with long, stiff bristles, available in several widths.

POUNCING. Paint or glaze is applied to a surface in a brisk up-and-down motion. This is one method of stenciling (page 119) that allows for easy blending of colors and shading. Pouncing is also the motion required for stippling.

REMOVAL TECHNIQUE. Some faux finishes are created by applying glaze to a surface and then partially removing it, using one tool or a combination of tools. A visual pattern or texture is developed as part of the base coat is revealed.

SKEWINGS. Excess scraps of metal leaf that are brushed away from the seams of a metal-leafing project may be used to fill in any open spaces. Skewings can also be used to create unique metallic effects (page 107).

SOFTEN. Brush-stroke lines or sharp contasts are eliminated by gently dabbing the surface with wadded cheesecloth. This motion breaks up the glaze slightly and also "pushes" details into the surface of the finish.

SPATTERING. A paint or other medium is applied to the surface in droplets by dipping a round artist's brush in the medium and tapping it while holding it above the surface. This technique is used for applying droplets of denatured alcohol to the surface for faux lapis (page 61) or faux travertine (page 81).

SPECKING. Tiny specks of paint are applied to a surface, using a toothbrush. The bristle tips are dipped in diluted paint and blotted slightly to remove excess paint. While the toothbrush is held above the surface, with the front end pointing at the area to be specked, the index finger is pulled across the bristles from front to back. This motion flicks specks of paint at the surface.

STIPPLING. This technique is used to break up a glazed surface into a finely grained texture, eliminating brush strokes and allowing the base-coat color to show through. It can also be used to blend adjoining colors of glaze. Stipplers have stiff, natural bristles with slightly feathered tips. They are available in a variety of sizes, with either long handles or arranged in a hand-held block style. The stippling technique is a vertical pouncing over the surface, constantly changing the direction of the wrist, arm, and shoulder.

TROMPE L'OEIL is a French term meaning "deceive the eye." This style of faux finishing creates the illusion of reality. Highlighting, shadowing, and perspective techniques are used to develop depth and dimension, for a realistic appearance.

VEIN. Mineral infusions in marbles and stones appear as wavering networks of fine lines, varying in thickness and density. The veining patterns vary with the types of marbles and stones, and can therefore be imitated in faux finishing with a variety of tools and techniques.

WET EDGE. When a faux finish is applied to a large surface, small areas are worked at a time, keeping a narrow margin of glaze around the outer edge wet and undisturbed. Glaze is applied in adjoining areas up to this wet edge, and the finish is then worked from one area into the next, thus avoiding obvious seams.

WHISKING. A dry natural-bristle brush, such as a goat hair or badger blender, is lightly stroked across the surface to soften harsh edges, blend adjoining colors, or elongate lines or specks of glaze or paint. Whisking is a brisk, even motion from the elbow.

Wood-grain
Finishes
& More

BASIC WOOD-GRAINING TECHNIQUES

It is extremely helpful to study the wood-grain patterns in real woods when learning to copy them in paint. Realistic wood-grain finishes will typically require a combination of techniques, just as real woods exhibit a variety of different patterns. Three basic grain patterns found in most woods are straight grain, heart grain, and crotch grain. These grain lines are actually the tree's annual rings, cut lengthwise. Which pattern is revealed depends not only on the type of wood, but also on the part of the tree from which it was cut, and the way the tree grew.

Wood-grain patterns may be created using a choice of techniques or tools. The technique for applying straight grain, for example, is generally a combing (page 24) technique. However, the resulting straight grains have very different looks, depending on the tool that is used to comb the glazed surface. Heart grain may be created using an artist's paintbrush in an applied (page 24) technique, or using a wood-graining rocker in a removal (page 24) technique. Though the removal technique may seem easier, the applied technique allows the artist to create more realistic heart-grain patterns for specific types of wood. Crotch grain, usually seen upside down, is created using a combination of applied and removal techniques.

Subtle texture in wood graining that gives the finish a realistic appearance is called pore structure. Found only in hardwoods, pore structure is actually a sliced-open view of the cell construction of the tree. The appearance of pore structure differs among types of wood, and can therefore be imitated in different ways.

Straight grain results from wood that is quarter-sawn, meaning the tree trunk is cut lengthwise into quarters and boards are sawed from each quarter.

Heart grain is revealed when lengthwise cuts are made across the entire trunk width.

Crotch grain comes from a section of the tree where two limbs branched out from each other.

HOW TO APPLY A STRAIGHT-GRAIN PATTERN

MATERIALS

- Glaze in desired color; desired applicator for applying glaze.

- Removal tools, such as triangular rubber comb, steel combs, cheesecloth, bristle overgrainer, or flogger; cotton-tipped swabs, artist's eraser, or wipe-out tool.

1 Apply glaze to surface, stroking in desired direction of wood grain. Drag rubber comb through glaze in parallel strokes, following direction of the grain and removing glaze. Begin and end each stroke just beyond the surface area; wipe glaze from tool after each stroke. Alternate sides of comb for variation.

2 Drag two cotton-tipped swabs together through dark stripes, breaking up into smaller, irregular stripes; allow hand to waver slightly in a few stripes. Repeat in some areas with corner of artist's eraser or wipe-out tool, creating a few finer stripes.

STRAIGHT-GRAIN VARIATIONS

Cheesecloth. Wrap fingers with two layers of cheesecloth; drag over glazed surface in direction of grain, lifting glaze in wide stripes. Vary width of stripes by spreading fingers or pulling fingers closer together in subsequent rows.

Flogger. Place flogger bristles flat on surface; drag through wet glaze, creating very subtle straight grain.

Bristled overgrainer. Drag overgrainer through wet glaze, creating soft, wide stripes **(a).** Or dip overgrainer in glaze and apply stripes to surface **(b).** Slight wavering of hand gives grain a more realistic appearance.

Steel combs. Drag combs quickly through wet glaze in repeated up-and-down strokes, combing over area to achieve desired grain pattern.

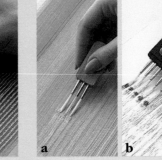

a   b

HOW TO APPLY A HEART-GRAIN PATTERN
USING AN ARTIST'S BRUSH

MATERIALS

- Glaze in desired color.
- Artist's brush, such as dagger or liner.
- Blending brush.

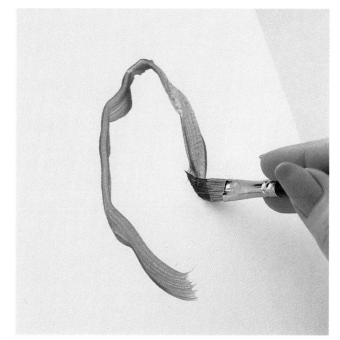

1 Apply center heart-grain line fairly wide, using desired artist's brush; paint oval-shaped line with irregularly spaced peaks.

2 Whisk heart-grain pattern lightly, using blending brush and following direction of the grain. This softens and elongates grain lines.

3 Apply two or three lines outside the center line; each new line should be thinner than the center and vaguely echo the pattern of the center. Whisk.

4 Apply thin grain lines on both sides of heart-grain lines; bend lines inward at outer ends of heart and extend to edge of surface or into next heart-grain pattern. Whisk.

HOW TO APPLY A HEART-GRAIN PATTERN USING A WOOD-GRAINING ROCKER

- Glaze in desired color; desired applicator for applying glaze.
- Wood-graining rocker.
- Blending brush.

1 Apply glaze to surface, stroking in desired direction of wood grain. Slide wood-graining rocker through wet glaze, rocking it slowly to create heart-grain effect. Start at one end, working in one continuous motion as you slide and rock the tool toward the opposite end. As you rock the tool, oval markings are created. (Position of rocker corresponds to markings of heart grain, as shown above.) Follow step 2 on page 31 to soften and elongate lines.

HOW TO APPLY A CROTCH-GRAIN PATTERN

- Glaze in desired color.
- Foam applicator, 1" (2.5 cm) wide.
- Cheesecloth.

1 Apply glaze to surface, using foam applicator; begin strokes at center of surface and arc downward toward outer edges at sharp angles. Alternate strokes on either side of center until entire surface is covered with glaze; allow some areas to be lighter than others.

2 Wad cheesecloth. Wipe surface with cheesecloth, beginning stroke with shallow hook near center and stroking downward at a sharp angle. Alternate strokes from left to right side of center, staggering tops of strokes opposite each other. Sides should not be mirror images of each other. Rewad cheesecloth as necessary.

HOW TO APPLY PORE STRUCTURE

MATERIALS

- Toothbrush and blending brush, for specking method.
- Flogger, for flogging method.
- Foam applicator and check roller, for oak method.

Specking method. Speck (page 25) surface in desired areas with diluted paint, using toothbrush. Whisk (page 25) specks, if desired, using blending brush.

Flogging method. Flog (page 24) glazed surface, holding flogger bristles parallel to surface.

1 Oak method. Dip foam applicator in glaze. Position applicator over check roller so foam rubs on metal wheels; hold both tools together.

2 Roll check roller up surface in straight, parallel lines, creating tiny vertical dashes. Reload foam applicator as needed.

FAUX ZEBRAWOOD FINISH

Zebrawood is a valuable wood grown in Africa. It has a straight grain of thin parallel stripes with a fine pore structure of tiny specks in some stripes and tiny streaks in others. Ribbons of slightly darker

Genuine zebrawood.

and lighter tones, each covering several rows of stripes, break up the otherwise uniform appearance of zebrawood.

MATERIALS

- Pale tan low-luster latex enamel paint, for base coat; sponge applicator, roller, or paintbrush.
- Dark brown satin glaze (page 14); sponge applicator.
- Cheesecloth; cotton-tipped swabs; artist's eraser or wipe-out tool.
- Dark brown wash (page 14).
- Toothbrush; blending brush.
- Satin clear finish or aerosol satin clear acrylic sealer.

HOW TO APPLY A FAUX ZEBRAWOOD FINISH

1 Prepare surface (page 18). Apply base coat of pale tan low-luster latex enamel to surface, using applicator suitable to size of surface. Allow to dry. Apply dark brown glaze to surface, using sponge applicator and stroking in desired direction of wood grain.

2 Create straight grain, using cheesecloth method on page 30. Follow step 2 on page 30 to break up the pattern into smaller stripes. Allow to dry.

3 Paint pore structure, using the specking method on page 33 with dark brown diluted paint. Concentrate specks more heavily in some stripes than others. Whisk narrow bands of specks, stroking either up or down in the direction of grain. Leave alternate bands of specks undisturbed. Allow to dry.

4 Apply dark brown wash to the surface. Drag surface in direction of grain with wadded cheesecloth, removing more wash in bands of unwhisked specks, and leaving whisked bands slightly darker. Allow to dry. Apply several thin coats of satin clear finish or aerosol satin clear acrylic sealer, allowing surface to dry between coats.

FAUX OAK FINISH

Oak is a very common hardwood, used for centuries in furniture and architecture. Its popularity results not only from its strength and durability, but also from its distinctive straight and heart-grain patterns. The straight-grain pattern of quarter-sawn oak may exhibit light-reflective pale streaks known as ray flecks. Oak also has a unique pore structure that appears as tiny slits in the wood.

When applying faux oak or any faux wood finish, keep in mind

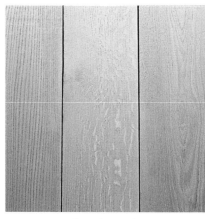

Genuine oak.

that real boards and veneers are limited in width. For a realistic finish and for ease of application, divide the base-coated surface into sections. Mask off alternate sections, and apply the graining steps of the finish to all the exposed sections. Remove the masking tape from each section as the steps are completed. When completely dry, mask off the grained sections and repeat the same steps for the remaining exposed sections. Apply the final steps to the entire surface.

HOW TO APPLY A FAUX OAK FINISH

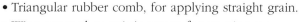

MATERIALS

- Pale tan low-luster latex enamel paint, for base coat; sponge applicator, roller, or paintbrush.
- Painter's masking tape.
- Medium brown satin glaze (page 14).
- Artist's brush, such as dagger or liner, for applying heart grain in applied method; or wood-graining rocker, for applying heart grain in removal method.
- Blending brush.

- Triangular rubber comb, for applying straight grain.
- Wipe-out tool or artist's eraser, for creating ray flecks.
- Check roller; sponge applicator in same width as check roller.
- Medium brown wash (page 14); foam applicator; cheesecloth.
- Satin clear finish or aerosol satin clear acrylic sealer.

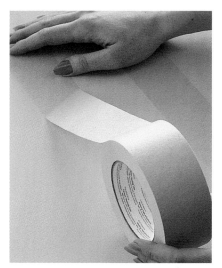

1 Prepare the surface (page 18). Apply a base coat of pale tan low-luster latex enamel to surface, using applicator suitable to size of surface. Allow to dry. Divide the surface and mask off sections as described opposite.

2 Apply heart grain to the desired sections of surface, using either method on pages 31 and 32. Apply straight grain to the desired sections, following steps 1 and 2 on page 33. Whisk (page 25) the surface, using blending brush to soften grain lines.

3 Remove narrow, short streaks of glaze in some sections of straight grain to create ray flecks, using wipe-out tool or corner of artist's eraser. Ray-fleck pattern should have a general diagonal flow; individal flecks may be slightly curved in one direction. Remove tape; allow to dry.

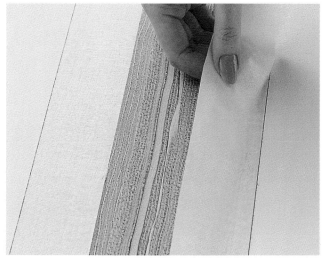

4 Mask off grained sections, positioning tape so that hairline of glaze is exposed. Repeat steps 2 and 3. Apply pore structure to entire surface, using the oak method on page 33. Allow to dry.

5 Apply medium brown wash to surface; dab with wadded cheesecloth to soften. Allow to dry. Apply several coats of satin clear finish, allowing surface to dry between coats.

FAUX MAHOGANY FINISH

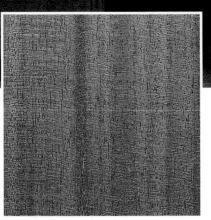

Genuine mahogany.

Mahogany, grown in tropical forests in several areas of the world, has long been a popular wood for cabinetry and fine furniture. Many varieties of mahogany exist, ranging in color from golden brown to dark reddish brown.

Crotch-grain mahogany, perhaps one of the most dramatic woods, is a favorite veneer for inset panels on doors or drawer fronts. The straight-grain pattern of mahogany appears as wide ribbons of light and dark shadow, with a highly textured underlying pore structure.

HOW TO APPLY A FAUX MAHOGANY FINISH

MATERIALS

- Light reddish brown low-luster latex enamel paint, for base coat; sponge applicator, roller, or paintbrush.
- Painter's masking tape.
- Burnt umber satin glaze (page 14).
- Cheesecloth; blending brush; flogger.
- Satin clear finish or aerosol satin clear acrylic sealer.

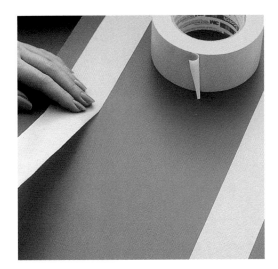

1 Prepare the surface (page 18). Apply base coat of light reddish brown low-luster latex enamel to surface, using applicator suitable to size of surface. Allow to dry. Divide surface and mask off sections (page 36) as necessary.

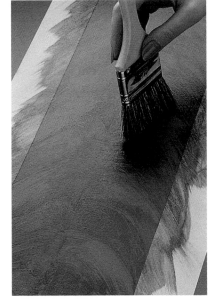

2 Apply crotch-grain pattern to desired sections, using burnt umber glaze and following steps 1 and 2 on page 32. Whisk (page 25) surface toward the center, using blending brush and following the angle of strokes. Add more glaze to darken the center, if necessary; whisk. Remove tape; allow to dry.

3 Apply glaze to section that will be painted with straight grain. Apply pore structure, using flogging method on page 33. Allow to dry slightly. Whisk surface perpendicular to desired grain line, using blending brush. Allow to dry. Repeat for remaining exposed straight-grain sections.

4 Apply straight-grain pattern, using the cheesecloth method on page 30, and leaving fairly wide bands of glaze. Dab with wadded cheesecloth to soften. Repeat for the remaining exposed straight-grain sections. Remove tape; allow to dry.

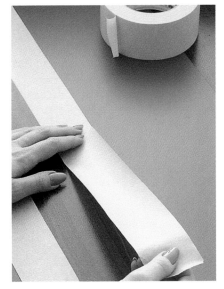

5 Mask off completed sections, positioning the tape so that hairline of the glaze is exposed. Repeat steps 2 to 4 for sections as desired. Apply several coats of satin clear finish, allowing the surface to dry between coats.

FAUX SATINWOOD FINISH

Satinwood is a lustrous yellow wood with a compact, smooth texture. Though grain lines are very faint in satinwood, the surface has an eye-catching changeable luster. This is caused by a twisting of the compact cell structure, which reflects light in undulating waves.

MATERIALS

- Pale yellow low-luster latex enamel paint, for base coat; sponge applicator, roller, or paintbrush.
- Painter's masking tape.
- Raw sienna satin glaze (page 14).
- Raw sienna wash (page 14).

- Artist's brush, such as dagger or liner, for painting heart grain in applied method; or wood-graining rocker for painting heart grain in removal method.
- Blending brush, flogger.
- Satin clear finish or aerosol clear acylic sealer.

Genuine satinwood.

HOW TO APPLY A FAUX SATINWOOD FINISH

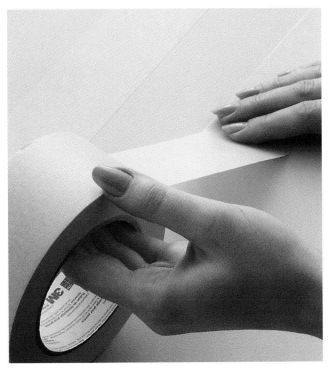

1 Prepare the surface (page 18). Apply base coat of pale yellow low-luster latex enamel to surface, using applicator suitable to size of surface. Allow to dry. Divide the surface and mask off sections as described on page 36.

2 Apply heart grain to desired sections of the surface, using raw sienna satin glaze; use either method on pages 31 and 32. Keep the grain lines as minimal and thin as possible.

3 Apply straight grain to the desired sections, following flogger method on page 30. Whisk scattered areas of the surface perpendicular to straight grain, blurring lines. Remove tape; allow to dry.

4 Mask off glazed sections, positioning the tape so that hairline of glaze is exposed. Repeat steps 2 and 3. Apply raw sienna wash to surface; roll tightly twisted, damp cheesecloth over the surface, partially removing wash in uneven pattern. Allow to dry. Apply several coats of satin clear finish, allowing the surface to dry between coats.

FAUX BIRD'S-EYE
MAPLE FINISH

Bird's-eye maple is a beautiful light-colored wood with many fine details, most obvious of which are the scattered oval markings that resemble tiny bird's eyes. This wood is also marked by very fine, wavering grain lines and a subtle, wavy reflection of light across the surface.

Because of the intricate detail work in the bird's-eye maple finish, it is most suitable for accessories and small surface areas of furniture.

Genuine bird's-eye maple.

MATERIALS

- Rich cream low-luster latex enamel paint, for base coat; sponge applicator, roller, or paintbrush.
- Light brown wash (page 14).
- Light brown satin glaze (page 14).
- Cheesecloth; overgrainer; cotton-tipped swabs; handle of small artist's paintbrush.
- Hand-held hair dryer.
- Satin clear finish or aerosol satin clear acrylic sealer.

HOW TO APPLY A
FAUX BIRD'S-EYE MAPLE FINISH

1 Prepare the surface (page 18). Apply base coat of rich cream low-luster latex enamel to surface, using applicator suitable to size of surface. Allow to dry. Apply light brown wash to surface, using sponge applicator. Dab with wadded cheesecloth to soften. Allow to dry.

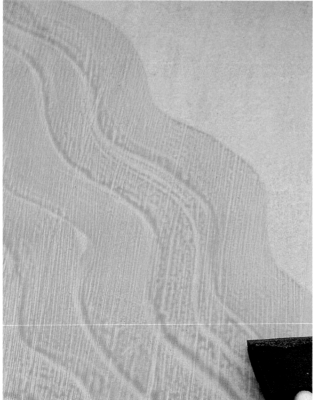

2 Apply wash to surface in wavy, diagonal streaks, using sponge applicator. Allow to dry only slightly.

3 Blow surface with hand-held hair dryer, forcing some of the wet wash to spread out in little streams across the surface. Allow to dry thoroughly.

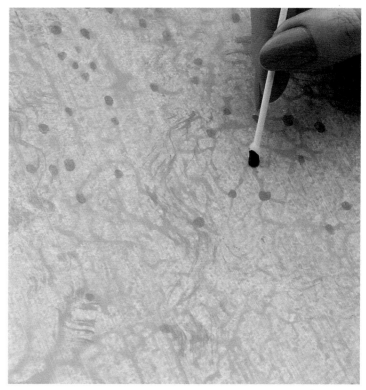

4 Apply straight-grain pattern in some areas, using bristled overgrainer method (b) on page 30 and light brown glaze. Separate bristles of overgrainer with hair comb to make finer lines; waver hand, generally following erratic pattern of wash lines. Allow to dry.

5 Remove some cotton from end of cotton-tipped swab. Dip tip in light brown glaze; touch tip to the surface, dragging slightly upward as tip is lifted from surface to create oval dot. Repeat for all bird's-eye markings within a small area. Apply markings alone or in small clusters, avoiding any regular pattern. Allow markings to dry only slightly.

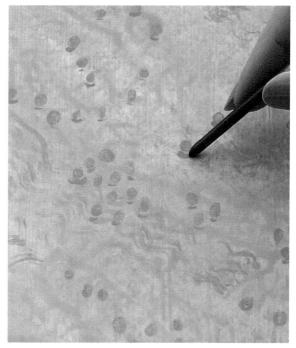

6 Blot markings with damp wadded cheese-cloth, absorbing some of the glaze, and leaving oval, outlined shadows.

7 Repeat steps 5 and 6 for entire surface. Dip tip of artist's paintbrush handle into glaze; apply tiny arc of glaze at lower edge of oval marking. Repeat for all markings. Allow to dry. Apply several thin coats of satin clear finish or aerosol satin clear acrylic sealer, allowing surface to dry between coats.

FAUX TIGER MAPLE FINISH

Another maple with an intricate grain pattern is tiger maple, also called curly maple. It also has wavering grain lines, much like bird's-eye maple, but without the oval markings.

The most striking characteristic of this wood is a pronounced striping perpendicular to the grain lines. These stripes, which look much like the stripes of a tiger, are caused by a twisting and waving of the grain as the tree grows. Light is reflected off the surface at different angles, setting up the striped pattern.

Genuine tiger maple.

MATERIALS

- Rich cream low-luster latex enamel paint, for base coat; sponge applicator, roller, or paintbrush.
- Tan wash (page 14).
- Cheesecloth; overgrainer; hand-held hair dryer.
- Burnt sienna urethane glaze (page 14).
- Turkey feather.
- Satin clear finish or aerosol clear acrylic sealer.

HOW TO APPLY A FAUX TIGER MAPLE FINISH

1 Follow steps 1 to 4 on page 44. Cut the vane on the convex side of turkey feather to within ¼" (6 mm) of quill.

2 Apply urethane glaze to surface. Holding the cut edge of feather perpendicular to vertical grain, push glaze in waves from one end of the surface to the other, creating striped pattern.

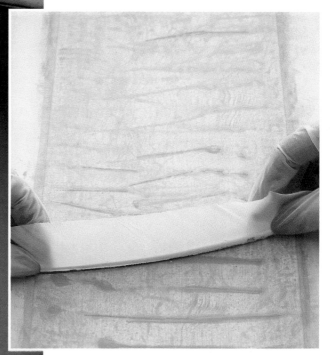

3 Change angle of feather to slightly less than perpendicular to vertical grain. Push glaze back in waves, moving in the opposite direction and breaking up striped pattern created in step 2. Allow to dry. Apply several thin coats of satin clear finish or aerosol clear acrylic sealer, allowing surface to dry between coats.

FAUX BURLED WOOD FINISH

Burled wood is cut from an erratic growth on the outer surface of a tree trunk where numerous small branch buds have grown together into a large clump. Though burled wood lacks strength, its dramatic texture makes it suitable for decorative veneer applications on furniture. Burled wood may come from one of several tree sources. To create a burled wood finish, select colors for the base coat and glaze to match the finish on the other parts of the furniture piece, or select a combination that will give the desired finish.

Genuine burled wood.

MATERIALS

- Low-luster latex enamel paint in desired color, for base coat; sponge applicator, paintbrush, or roller.
- Glaze in desired color; sponge applicator.
- Cheesecloth; small stencil brush; blending brush.
- Satin clear finish or aersol satin clear acrylic sealer.

HOW TO APPLY A FAUX BURLED WOOD FINISH

1 Prepare surface (page 18). Mask off any adjoining areas of surface. Apply base coat of desired color low-luster latex enamel, using applicator suitable to size of surface. Allow to dry. Apply ample amount of glaze to the surface, using sponge applicator; apply glaze in short strokes in random directions. Dab with wadded cheesecloth to soften.

2 Form the cheesecloth into small ball; rub lightly through the glaze in short swirls of varying sizes and directions. Whisk (page 25) the surface very lightly, if necessary.

3 Dip tip of small stencil brush into glaze; add dark dot to center of a swirl, with single pounce and slight twist of brush. Repeat for other swirls as desired, clumping dark dots in some areas for erratic appearance.

4 Remove any masking tape. Allow to dry. Apply several thin coats of satin clear finish or aersol satin clear acrylic sealer, allowing surface to dry between coats.

FAUX BONE & HORN FINISHES

Inlaid accents of bone and horn may be found in some antique furniture or accessories. Bone and horn have also been used to make jewelry items, such as beads, bracelets, and earrings. The two materials are very similar in texture, though they differ in color. Bone is ivory in color, with streaks and specks of gray and brown tones. Horn is usually dark brown in color, with streaks of lighter earth-tone colors.

To achieve the look of natural bone and horn, earth-tone paints are applied, using simple techniques of specking and blending (pages 25 and 24). Because bones and horns are naturally small in size, suitable surfaces for faux bone and horn finishes are also relatively small and the finishes are generally applied in small, abutting sections as if they were pieced together. The naturally occurring grain lines in bone or horn run lengthwise

Genuine bone and horn.

through each section. Sections may be arranged so that all grain lines run in the same direction, or some sections may be turned at opposing angles to add interest.

MATERIALS

- Low-luster latex enamel paint, for base coat; use white for bone finish, black for horn finish.
- Sponge applicator or paintbrush.
- Painter's masking tape.
- Acrylic paints in white, black, and earth-tone colors, such as raw sienna, burnt sienna, raw umber, and burnt umber.
- Round artist's brush; cheesecloth; blending brush; toothbrush; paper towels.
- High-gloss clear finish or aerosol high-gloss clear acrylic sealer.

HOW TO APPLY A FAUX BONE FINISH

1 Prepare surface (page 18). Apply base coat of white low-luster latex enamel to surface, using sponge applicator or paintbrush. Allow to dry.

2 Divide the surface into narrow rectangular sections of various sizes, with light pencil lines. Mask off alternate sections of surface so that exposed sections have no shared lines. Burnish (page 24) tape edges. Thin black and several earth-tone colors of acrylic paints with equal parts water in separate containers.

(Continued)

3 Apply streaks of desired colors throughout section, using round artist's brush; concentrate darker streaks along outer edges, curving streaks slightly inward at top and bottom.

4 Dab with wadded cheesecloth to soften and blend slightly. Whisk with blending brush, following the direction of streaks. Allow to dry.

5 Dip toothbrush in desired color of thinned paint; blot lightly on paper towel. Speck (page 25) along outer edges of section.

6 Whisk over specks in direction of streaks, using blending brush and stroking only in one direction.

7 Repeat steps 5 and 6 with additional colors as desired. Apply additional fine spatters in desired colors throughout section; do not whisk. Allow to dry.

8 Repeat steps 3 to 7 for each exposed section; sections may differ in color and amount of specking. Run all grain lines in the same direction or change the direction of some sections, if desired. Allow to dry. Remove tape.

9 Mask off painted sections, positioning tape so that hairline of paint is exposed. Paint remaining sections, following steps 3 to 7. Remove tape. Apply several thin coats of high-gloss clear finish or aerosol high-gloss clear acrylic sealer, allowing surface to dry between coats.

HOW TO APPLY A FAUX HORN FINISH

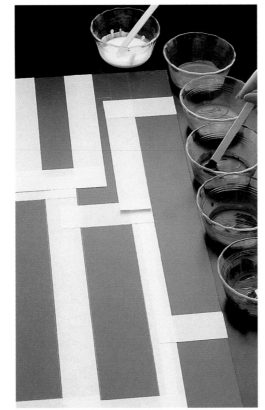

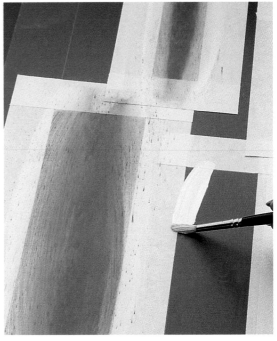

1 Follow steps 1 and 2 on page 51, using black low-luster latex enamel for base coat. Thin white and several colors of earth-tone acrylic paints with equal parts water in separate containers.

2 Apply streaks of desired colors throughout section, using round artist's brush; concentrate lighter streaks along outer edges, bending streaks slightly inward at top and bottom. Follow steps 4 to 9, above, omitting fine specks in step 7.

FAUX TIGEREYE FINISH

Tigereye is a semiprecious stone often used in jewelry or small ornamental pieces. This dark, glassy stone is characterized by undulating narrow bands of gold that have a changeable luster, like the eye of a cat.

The gold bands of a faux tigereye finish are created by first covering the surface with gold leaf (page 100). A raw umber gloss glaze is applied over the leafed surface and combed (page 24), using the notched edge of an eraser, to reveal irregular bands of gold. After drying, a wash (page 14) is drawn across the bands in the opposite direction, forming shadowy streaks that give the tigereye its undulating quality. A high-gloss finish is an essential last step, giving the tigereye finish a glassy brilliance.

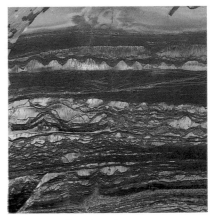

Genuine tigereye.

Tigereye finish is appropriate for small, flat surfaces, such as a wooden box lid or picture frame. For an inlaid effect, a border of tigereye finish can be applied around the outer edge of a small table or tray.

HOW TO APPLY A FAUX TIGEREYE FINISH

MATERIALS

- Acrylic or latex paint in gold color, for base coat; sponge applicator.
- 400-grit wet/dry sandpaper; damp cloth.
- Water-based gold-leaf adhesive size; sponge applicator or soft-bristled paintbrush.
- Composition gold leaf; scissors; thin cotton gloves, optional.
- Soft paintbrush, 1" (2.5 cm) wide, for tamping and smoothing gold leaf.

- Clear finish or aerosol clear acrylic sealer.
- Soft artist's eraser; mat knife.
- Raw umber gloss glaze (page 14); sponge applicator or paintbrush; newspaper.
- Cheesecloth.
- Raw umber wash (page 14).
- High-gloss clear finish or aerosol high-gloss clear acrylic sealer.

1 Prepare the surface and apply gold leaf, as in steps 1 to 9, pages 100 to 103. Notch edges of eraser in irregular pattern, using mat knife. Test the notch patterns by pulling eraser edges through thin glaze spread on tagboard scrap. Each notched edge should leave clean, irregularly spaced stripes of varying widths from pencil-line thin to ¼" (6 mm) wide. Adjust notches, if necessary.

(Continued)

2 Apply the glaze to leafed surface, using sponge applicator or paintbrush; draw brush across surface in parallel lines.

3 Comb through the glaze in direction of brush strokes, using the notched edge of the eraser. Start at outer edge of the surface; move eraser slowly from top to bottom in a continuous motion, creating gold bands with irregular small waves, dips, and peaks. Wipe excess glaze from eraser onto newspaper.

4 Comb through glaze next to previous bands, using another notched edge of eraser; vaguely follow pattern of previous bands. Wipe excess glaze from eraser. Repeat until entire surface has been combed, varying width of bands and spaces between them.

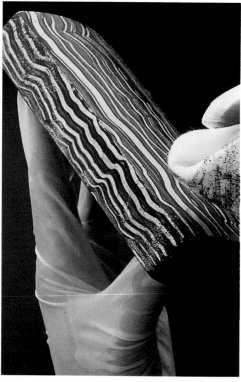

5 Dab surface with wadded cheesecloth, slightly softening gold bands. Allow to dry thoroughly.

6 Apply wash to the surface with paintbrush, stroking in direction perpendicular to gold bands and making wash more visible in some areas than others; allow hand to tremble, creating shadowy streaks. Allow to dry thoroughly.

7 Apply several thin coats of high-gloss clear finish or aerosol high-gloss clear acrylic sealer, allowing the surface to dry between coats.

HOW TO APPLY AN INLAID TIGEREYE DESIGN

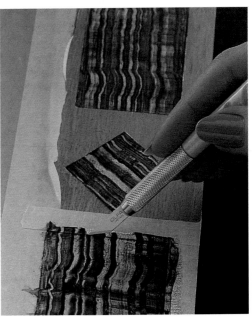

1 Prepare surface as in steps 1 and 2 on page 102. Mask off the design area, using painter's masking tape. Apply gold leaf as in steps 3 to 8 on pages 102 and 103.

2 Follow steps 2 to 6, opposite. Score inlaid design along edges of the tape, using mat knife. Remove tape carefully. Apply several thin coats of high-gloss clear finish or aerosol high-gloss clear acrylic sealer to entire surface, allowing surface to dry between coats.

FAUX LAPIS FINISH

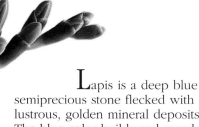

Genuine lapis.

L apis is a deep blue semiprecious stone flecked with lustrous, golden mineral deposits. The blue color builds and recedes in drifts, in spots revealing pale gray tones. Because of its scarcity, it is generally used in fine jewelry or small, ornate accessories.

Faux lapis is applied using a stippling technique (page 25). Two different deep blue paint glazes are stippled onto the surface in diagonal drifts, sometimes blending with each other and at other times remaining separate, thus creating the characteristic depth of color. Droplets of denatured alcohol, spattered over the wet glaze, cause amorphous rings in the glaze. Gold powder is sprinkled over the wet glaze and gently pressed into the surface to resemble mineral deposits. After drying, a high-gloss aerosol acrylic sealer is applied for a glassy appearance.

For a realistic appearance, faux lapis can be applied to any small paintable surface, such as a ceramic vase. It can also be applied as inlaid sections on a flat surface.

When using metallic powders, avoid any drafts that may blow the powder around and wear a protective mask to prevent inhaling the fine particles.

MATERIALS

- Light gray low-luster latex enamel paint, for base coat; sponge applicator or paintbrush.
- Prussian blue gloss glaze (page 14).
- Cobalt blue gloss glaze (page 14).
- Stippler, in size suitable to project.
- Denatured alcohol; round artist's paintbrush.
- Cheesecloth.
- Gold powder; protective mask.
- Aerosol high-gloss clear acrylic sealer.

HOW TO APPLY A FAUX LAPIS FINISH

1 Prepare the surface (page 18). Apply base coat of light gray low-luster latex enamel to the surface, using sponge applicator or paintbrush. Allow to dry.

2 Apply Prussian blue glaze in random strokes, using sponge applicator or paintbrush; cover about half the surface. Repeat with cobalt blue glaze in remaining areas; leave some small areas of base coat unglazed.

(Continued)

3 Stipple (page 25) over entire area, blending colors slightly and leaving lighter small areas where base coat shows through.

4 Spatter (page 25) droplets of denatured alcohol over wet glaze, using round artist's paint-brush; apply droplets in diagonal drifts. Allow alcohol to react in the glaze.

5 Dab some alcohol droplets with wadded cheesecloth to soften; leave other droplets undisturbed.

6 Apply more Prussian blue glaze onto the surface in diagonal drifts; repeat, using cobalt blue glaze. Stipple, blending colors slightly. Repeat steps 4 and 5.

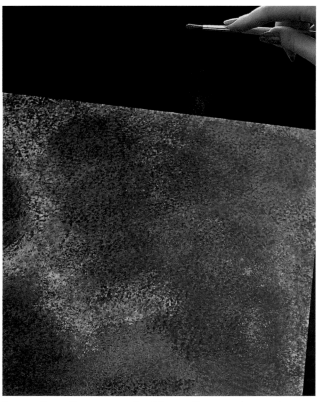

7 Load small amount of gold metallic powder on dry round paintbrush. Hold brush about 12" (30.5 cm) above surface; tap brush gently, allowing powder to fall onto darker areas of surface in small concentrations.

8 Press gold powder gently into surface with wadded cheesecloth.

9 Repeat steps 7 and 8 as desired. Apply more Prussian blue glaze in some areas, deepening color; soften with cheesecloth. Repeat step 4 over fresh glaze. Allow the entire surface to dry thoroughly.

10 Apply several thin coats of aerosol high-gloss clear acrylic sealer, allowing surface to dry between coats.

The distinctive banding pattern and vibrant green color of malachite make this semiprecious stone instantly recognizable. A cross section of malachite reveals egg-shaped nodules surrounded by multiple bands, varying in width and intensity, that seem to echo from the nodules like ripples of water. Just as the surface of an egg has curves of varying degrees, the bands of malachite will vary from nearly straight to sharply curved. Genuine malachite in solid form is used in jewelry and carved objects, while thin slices of the stone are often inlaid in mosaic fashion on tabletops or other flat surfaces.

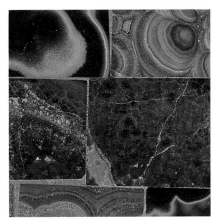

Genuine malachite.

The painting technique used to simulate malachite is combing (page 24), using an irregularly notched edge of an artist's eraser. Malachite is usually depicted as pieced geometric sections on a flat surface, with the banding direction changing at each adjoining line. Some sections may show a partial nodule, created by combing in a tight, oval shape, with surrounding bands that echo from the nodule. Other sections may contain only bands with varying degrees of curve. The bands often have a characteristic V-formation, created by combing in an arc, hesitating, and then changing direction into a new arc. It is helpful to sketch the layout of the sections and the pattern of banding in each section before beginning to paint. Also, practice the combing method to achieve the look of genuine malachite. Realistic applications of faux malachite include small-scale flat surfaces, such as trays or small tabletops, or inlaid sections on cabinet doors or drawer fronts. A final high-gloss finish gives faux malachite its characteristic depth and luster.

MATERIALS

- Paper and pencil, for sketching design.
- White low-luster latex enamel paint, for base coat; sponge applicator or paintbrush.
- Bright green or blue-green latex or craft acrylic paint and acrylic urethane, for urethane glaze.
- Painter's masking tape.
- Very dark hunter or forest green gloss glaze (page 14).
- Sponge applicator or paintbrush, for applying glazes.
- Soft artist's eraser; mat knife or razor blade.
- Newspaper; cheesecloth.
- Denatured alcohol; round artist's paintbrush.
- High-gloss clear finish or aerosol high-gloss clear acrylic sealer.

URETHANE GLAZE

Mix together the following ingredients:

One part bright green or blue-green latex paint or craft acrylic paint.

One part acrylic urethane.

One part water.

MAKING A SKETCH OF THE DESIGN

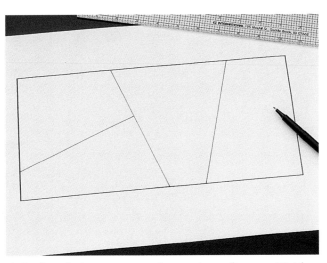

1 Outline design area to scale on piece of paper. Divide design area into sections, avoiding acute and square angles whenever possible.

2 Sketch banding pattern in each section, including partial nodules in some sections; vary banding direction and degree of curve in adjoining sections.

1 Prepare surface (page 18). Apply base coat of white low-luster latex enamel to the surface, using sponge applicator. Allow to dry.

2 Mix urethane glaze (page 65); apply to entire design area, using sponge applicator or paintbrush. Brush entire area, first in one direction and then in opposite direction, leveling glaze. Allow to dry thoroughly.

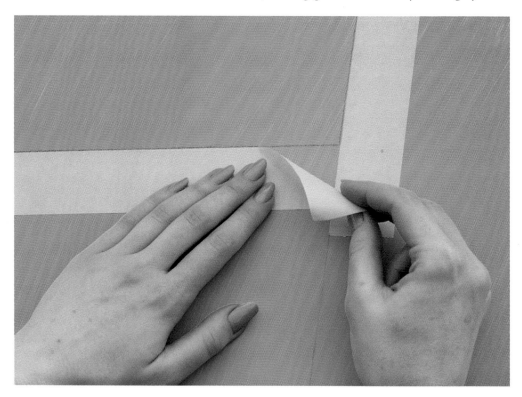

3 Divide the design area into sections with light pencil lines, following the sketch. Mask off first section to be glazed. Notch eraser edges as in step 1 on page 57.

4 Apply very dark green glaze to first design section, using sponge applicator or paintbrush. Comb notched eraser edge through glaze, following sketched banding pattern, beginning and ending combing motion just beyond design area. If the pattern contains a nodule, comb it first. Allow hand to waver occasionally. Wipe excess glaze from the eraser onto newspaper.

5 Comb through glaze next to previous bands, using another notched edge of eraser; follow pattern of previous bands, gradually widening arc on curved banding patterns. Repeat until section is completely combed. Remove tape.

6 Mask off next section that does not adjoin previously glazed section. Apply glaze; comb, following sketch. Remove tape. Repeat for remaining sections that do not adjoin. Allow to dry.

(Continued)

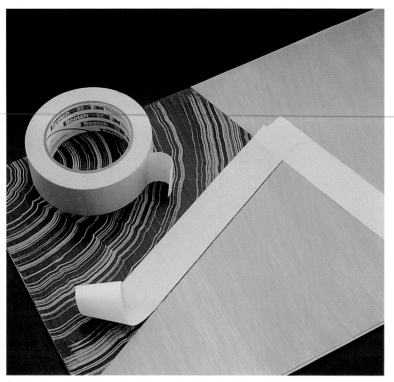

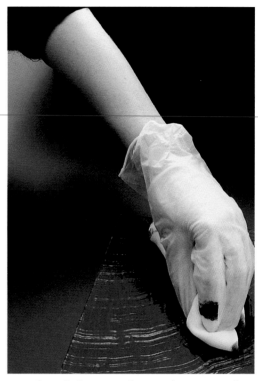

7 Mask off a section that adjoins a previously glazed section; position tape edge so hairline of glazed section is exposed. Apply the glaze; comb, following sketch. Remove tape. Repeat for remaining unglazed sections until design is complete. Allow to dry.

8 Dilute dark green glaze with water to the consistency of wash (page 14). Apply over entire design; dab with wadded cheesecloth to soften.

9 Spatter (page 25) immediately with denatured alcohol, using round paintbrush in random, sparse application. Allow to dry thoroughly.

10 Apply several thin coats of high-gloss clear finish or aerosol high-gloss clear acrylic sealer, allowing the surface to dry between coats.

FAUX PORTORO FINISH

Portoro, also known as black and gold marble, has been used for centuries in architecture and for smaller-scale decorative work. It is characterized by networks of fibrous veining, usually 1" to 3" (2.5 to 7.5 cm) wide and running in very linear patterns through wide expanses of black marble. The veining networks are often gold in color, though the color can be more

Genuine Portoro.

off-white or beige. Distinctive white secondary veins intersect the networks at opposing angles, threading over or under the veining in staggered lines.

Select faux Portoro for a dramatic finish on a bathroom wall or fireplace surround. On a smaller scale, paint a faux Portoro finish on a table base or pedestal. Apply the finish with the veining networks running horizontally or vertically. If possible, turn the work so that you are working vertically from top to bottom, because the veining brush will be held at right angles to the veining network. Start and end veining networks off the surface, implying visually that they continue beyond the cut marble.

MATERIALS

- Black low-luster latex enamel paint, for base coat; sponge applicator or paintbrush, for small surface, or roller, for larger surface.
- Gold metallic acrylic paint and acrylic urethane, for gold veining glaze.
- Round artist's brush.
- White gloss glaze (page 14).
- Black wash (page 14).
- Cheesecloth.
- High-gloss clear finish or aerosol high-gloss clear acrylic sealer.

HOW TO APPLY A
FAUX PORTORO FINISH

GOLD VEINING GLAZE

Mix together the following ingredients:

One part gold metallic craft acrylic paint.

One part acrylic urethane.

One part water.

1 Prepare surface (page 18). Apply base coat of black low-luster latex enamel to surface, using applicator suitable to surface size. Allow to dry.

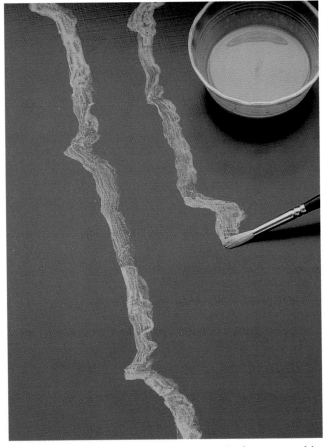

2 Mix gold veining glaze (above). Dip round artist's brush into water, then into glaze. Hold the brush sideways at upper edge of surface, at right angle to line of veining network; hold brush between thumb and fingers near end of handle, with thumb on top. Pull brush toward lower edge, rolling brush handle back and forth and fidgeting to create irregular, jagged veining line.

3 Repeat step 2 in second vein alongside first vein; add third vein as desired.

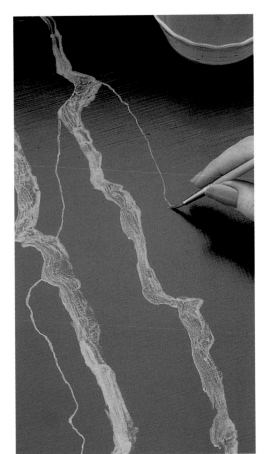

4 Dip the brush into water, then into the glaze. Paint thin, fidgety lines connecting adjacent veins, using the tip of the brush; also, form small nodules here and there along one side of each main vein by connecting jagged points.

5 Allow gold veining networks to dry. Dip the brush into water, then into white glaze. Paint a few thin, fidgety lines at opposing angles to the veining networks; avoid right angles. Cross directly over the top of some veining networks; on others break the white line as it passes behind gold veins. Allow to dry.

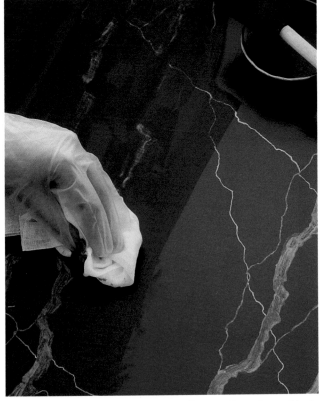

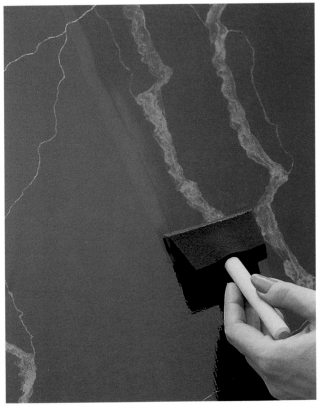

6 Apply black wash to entire surface. Dab with wadded cheesecloth to soften. Allow to dry.

7 Apply several thin coats of high-gloss clear finish or aerosol high-gloss clear acrylic sealer, allowing surface to dry between coats.

FAUX SERPENTINE FINISH

Serpentine is the general name given to a variety of green marbles that contain deposits of the mineral, serpentine. The different varieties vary in visual texture and color tone, often with traces of black and white. Some serpentines may be characterized by a network of fine veining, while others contain little or no veining. As with many marbles, the serpentines have various architectural uses, including floors, walls, and pillars.

Just as genuine marble is cut into workable pieces for installation, a faux serpentine finish applied to a large surface is more realistic if applied in sections with narrow grout lines (page 88). By masking off alternate sections, the finish can be applied to half the project, following steps 1 to 9. When the first half has been allowed to dry completely, the completed sections can be masked off, and the finish can be applied to the remaining sections. A high-gloss finish is then applied

Genuine serpentine.

to the entire surface, giving the faux finish the lustrous appearance of genuine serpentine marble.

MATERIALS

- Medium green low-luster latex enamel paint, for base coat; sponge applicator or paintbrush, for small surface, or low-napped roller, for larger surface.
- Black gloss glaze (page 14).
- Green gloss glaze (page 14), in darker shade than base coat.
- White gloss glaze (page 14).
- Newspaper, cheesecloth, stippler, for applying and working glaze.
- Spray bottle; water.
- Turkey feather, for veining.
- High-gloss clear finish or aerosol high-gloss clear acrylic sealer.

HOW TO APPLY A FAUX SERPENTINE FINISH

1 Prepare surface (page 18). Apply base coat of medium green low-luster latex enamel to surface, using applicator suitable to surface size.

2 Apply black, green, and white glazes separately in random, broad, diagonal strokes, using sponge applicator or paintbrush; cover most of the surface, allowing small patches of the base coat to show through.

(Continued)

3 Stipple (page 25) glazes in adjoining areas to blend slightly, using stippler.

4 Fold a sheet of newspaper to several layers; lay flat over an area of surface, in same diagonal direction as original strokes. Press newspaper into the glaze; lift, removing some of the glaze.

5 Repeat step 4 over the entire surface, using same newspaper; turn paper in opposite direction occasionally. Add glazes as desired to develop color. Dab areas of high contrast with wadded cheesecloth, to soften. Mist surface with water, if necessary, to keep glazes workable.

6 Brush black glaze onto newpaper and touch to the surface diagonally in scattered areas, adding drama and depth. Soften with cheesecloth, if necessary. Repeat, using white glaze in small, lighter areas.

7 Dilute mixture of white and green glazes with water to consistency of light cream. Run the edge and tip of the feather through diluted glaze. Place tip of feather onto surface in desired placement for vein; lightly drag feather diagonally over the surface, fidgeting and turning slightly and varying the pressure, to create irregular, jagged vein. Begin and end vein lines off edge of surface.

8 Repeat step 7 as desired to build veining pattern; connect adjacent vein lines occasionally, creating narrow, oblong, irregular shapes. Dab veins lightly with wadded cheesecloth to soften, if necessary. Allow surface to dry.

9 Dilute glazes to consistency of wash (page 14); apply randomly to surface. Dab with wadded cheesecloth to soften. Allow to dry.

10 Apply several thin coats of high-gloss clear finish or aerosol high-gloss clear acrylic sealer, allowing the surface to dry between coats.

FAUX NORWEGIAN ROSE FINISH

Norwegian rose is a white marble with patches of pink and green mineral deposits that give the marble its striking contrast of colors. Patchy drifts of dusty pink color fade into hues of taupe and tan, surrounded by a gray-green veining structure.

Genuine Norwegian rose.

The decorative uses for a faux Norwegian rose marble finish include floor or wall tiles, pillars, accessories, and tabletops. The marble pattern, determined by the direction of the veining structure, can be set up vertically, horizontally, or at an angle, depending on the desired effect.

MATERIALS

- White low-luster latex enamel paint, for base coat; sponge applicator or paintbrush, for small surface, or low-napped roller, for larger surface.
- White gloss glaze (page 14).

- Pink gloss glaze (page 14).
- Tan gloss glaze (page 14).
- Raw umber gloss glaze (page 14).

- Sponge applicator, cheesecloth, feather, blending brush, for applying and working glazes.
- White wash (page 14).
- High-gloss clear finish or aerosol high-gloss clear acrylic sealer.

HOW TO APPLY A
FAUX NORWEGIAN ROSE FINISH

1 Prepare surface (page 18). Apply base coat of white low-luster latex enamel to surface, using applicator suitable to surface size. Apply pink glaze to surface in a few random oval patches, angling ovals in desired direction of marble pattern.

2 Apply narrow patches of tan glaze along the sides of some pink patches, running tan areas together. Avoid any regular pattern or balanced placement. Apply white glaze in remaining areas. Dab with wadded cheesecloth to soften and blend adjoining colors.

3 Whisk (page 24) over surface in desired direction of the marble pattern, using blending brush to soften and elongate patches of color. Whisk occasionally in direction perpendicular to pattern to widen patches slightly.

4 Apply more glaze, dab with cheesecloth, and whisk as needed to achieve the desired look. Repeat for all areas of the surface.

5 Run edge and tip of feather through the raw umber glaze; drag the feather over the surface, creating vein lines and roughly outlining patches of color. Connect adjacent vein lines, creating narrow, oblong, irregular shapes.

6 Dab veins lightly with wadded cheesecloth to soften. Whisk with blending brush to elongate and blur vein lines. Allow to dry.

7 Apply white wash to the surface; dab with wadded cheesecloth to soften. Whisk with blending brush. Allow to dry. Apply several thin coats of high-gloss clear finish or aerosol high-gloss clear acrylic sealer, allowing the surface to dry between coats.

FAUX TRAVERTINE FINISH

Travertine is a type of limestone used extensively in architecture, especially for large surfaces such as floors and walls. It is formed when water from underground springs deposits layer upon layer of minerals in faulted horizontal bands. Throughout the layers of mineral deposits, small pits are created as the water evaporates. These open pits are very evident in unpolished travertine, the form used most often. For some uses of travertine, the surface pits are filled and the stone is polished. Because of its very linear structure, travertine can be used vertically, horizontally, or diagonally for different effects.

For a faux travertine finish, flat earth-tone glazes are applied in narrow, blended bands over a white base coat. Denatured alcohol is applied to the wet glaze, mottling the bands with swirls and voids that resemble the mineral deposits and pits in the stone. These mottled bands are separated by wide, pale bands that are very lightly streaked. When applying the finish to a large, unbroken surface, such as a wall or tabletop, apply all mottled bands first. Repeat steps 2 through 5 for each mottled band, working in rough 24" (61 cm) lengths and keeping a wet edge (page 25) until the entire band is complete. When all mottled bands are

Genuine travertine.

dry, apply thinned glaze, as in steps 7 and 8. Then apply all separating layers (steps 9 and 10). When all layers have been completed, the final wash and optional matte finish can be applied to the entire surface. The finish may also be applied in sections, resembling stone blocks (page 88), allowing you to work on one block at a time.

MATERIALS

- White low-luster latex enamel paint, for base coat; sponge applicator, paintbrush, or roller.
- Raw sienna flat glaze (page 14).
- Raw umber flat glaze (page 14).
- White flat glaze (page 14).
- Stippler.
- Spray bottle with water.
- Denatured alcohol; round artist's paintbrush.
- Cheesecloth.
- Blending brush.
- Ivory wash (page 14).
- Matte clear finish or aerosol matte clear acrylic sealer, optional.

HOW TO APPLY A FAUX TRAVERTINE FINISH

1 Prepare surface (page 18). Apply base coat of white low-luster latex enamel to surface, using applicator suitable to surface size. Allow to dry.

2 Apply narrow bands of raw sienna glaze, raw umber glaze, and white glaze next to each other on surface, breaking and staggering bands randomly.

(Continued)

3 Stipple (page 25) bands of glaze in adjoining areas, blending colors slightly. Mist with water to keep surface moist.

4 Dip round artist's paintbrush into denatured alcohol; touch tip of brush into wet glaze, applying small amounts of alcohol throughout stippled band. Reload brush as needed.

5 Roll brush through band, redistributing alcohol. Allow alcohol to react with glaze, creating swirls and voids throughout the band. Dab with cheesecloth as needed, to soften effect.

6 Repeat steps 2 through 5 for each mottled band, allowing spaces for separating bands three to four times the width of mottled band. Allow mottled bands to dry.

7 Thin white glaze with water to the consistency of light cream. Apply to mottled band, using sponge applicator or paintbrush; dab with wadded cheesecloth to soften.

8 Spatter (page 25) denatured alcohol throughout band; stipple. Add more thinned glaze as desired; repeat alcohol application.

9 Repeat steps 7 and 8 for each mottled band. Sideload the brush with small amount of raw umber glaze; dip into thinned white glaze. Draw brush through separating band several times, forming watery, pale streaks. Allow to dry slightly.

10 Whisk (page 25) over the slightly dry separating band with light strokes in the opposite direction, using dry blending brush.

11 Repeat steps 9 and 10 for all separating bands. Allow entire surface to dry thoroughly. Apply ivory wash, using sponge applicator or paintbrush; dab with wadded cheesecloth to soften. Allow to dry. Apply matte clear finish or aerosol matte clear acrylic sealer, if desired.

FAUX UNPOLISHED
STONE FINISH

Unpolished stone, in many colors and textures, is used extensively by the building industry, both in its natural state and cut into stone blocks. Just as genuine unpolished stones vary in surface textures, various faux painting techniques can be used to create faux unpolished stone finishes that are very different from each other.

The applied painting technique of stippling (page 25) results in a relatively smooth textured finish with blended colors. Another method, using newspaper in a combination of applied and removal techniques, results in a faux unpolished stone finish with depth and color variation.

Earth-tone glazes are used in all methods to create faux finishes that mimic real unpolished stones. Use the glazes suggested here, or select other earth-tone colors, as desired. For a faux finish resembling stone

Genuine unpolished stone.

blocks, mask off grout lines (page 88) and apply the finish to each block individually. This allows you to vary the depth of color in adjacent blocks. If applying the finish to a large undivided surface, work in smaller areas at a time, leaving a wet edge (page 25). When dry, the painted stone may be left unsealed, or sealed with a matte finish.

MATERIALS

- White low-luster latex enamel paint, for base coat; sponge applicator or paintbrush, for smaller surface; sponge or low-napped roller, for larger surface.
- Flat paint glazes (page 14) in a variety of earth-tone colors, black, and white.
- Stippler, for stippling method.
- Newspaper, for newspaper method.
- White wash; earth-tone wash (page 14); cheesecloth.
- Matte clear finish or aerosol matte clear acrylic sealer, optional.

HOW TO APPLY A FAUX UNPOLISHED STONE FINISH USING THE STIPPLING METHOD

1 Prepare the surface (page 18). Apply base coat of white low-luster latex enamel to the surface, using applicator suitable to surface size. Allow to dry. Mask off grout lines (page 88), if desired.

2 Apply flat earth-tone glaze in random strokes, using sponge applicator or paintbrush; cover about half the surface. Repeat with another color glaze in remaining areas; leave some small areas of base coat unglazed.

3 Stipple (page 25) over surface, using stippler; blend colors as desired, leaving some areas quite dark and others very light where base coat shows through. Add white and black glazes, if desired; add earth-tone glazes as necessary. Stipple to blend. Allow to dry.

4 Apply white wash to the entire surface. Dab with wadded cheesecloth to soften. Allow to dry. Apply matte clear finish or aerosol matte clear acrylic sealer, if desired.

HOW TO APPLY A FAUX UNPOLISHED STONE FINISH USING THE NEWSPAPER METHOD

1 Follow steps 1 and 2, opposite. Apply white wash in areas desired; apply earth-tone wash in areas desired.

2 Fold a sheet of newspaper to several layers. Lay it flat over one area of surface and press into glaze. Lift, removing some glaze. Repeat in other areas, turning same newspaper in different directions to blend colors roughly.

3 Add more color to an area by spreading glaze on newspaper and laying it flat on surface. Repeat as necessary until desired effect is achieved. Leave some dark accent areas in finish; also leave an occasional light spot. Use same newpaper throughout. Allow to dry.

4 Apply white wash to entire surface. Dab with wadded cheese-cloth to soften. Allow to dry. Apply matte clear finish or aerosol matte clear acrylic sealer, if desired.

GROUT LINES

Create the look of grouted marble tiles or stone blocks by masking off a grid on the base-coated surface before painting the faux finish. Grout lines can be simple and rough for a rustic look, or angle-cut at the corners and shaded for a trompe l'oeil effect.

For rustic grout lines, masking tape is applied to the surface, but not burnished (page 24). This allows some of the paint to seep under the tape edges, creating a slightly rough line. After the faux finish is applied, the tape is removed and the grout is painted in by hand, without caution or accuracy, thus creating the rustic look.

Trompe l'oeil grout lines are created by angle-cutting the intersections and burnishing the tape edges to ensure a crisp line. After applying the faux finish and before removing the tape, a marker in a shade darker than the base coat is used to draw in the shaded part of the grout.

Rustic grout lines are often used with highly textured unpolished stone or travertine finishes. The crisp lines of trompe l'oeil grout work well with marbles or finely textured unpolished stone.

MATERIALS

FOR RUSTIC GROUT
- ¼" (6 mm) masking tape.
- Round artist's brush.
- Glaze in shade to contrast with faux finish.

FOR TROMPE L'OEIL GROUT
- ⅛" (3 mm) masking tape, available at automotive supply stores.
- Mat knife.
- Burnishing tool, such as a plastic credit card.
- Flat-tipped marker in shade darker than base coat.

Trompe l'oeil grout lines, *above, help create the illusion of a Norwegian rose marble wall.*

Rustic grout lines, *opposite, separate the faux stone blocks for a deceiving floor finish.*

HOW TO APPLY RUSTIC GROUT LINES

1 Prepare the surface (page 18). Apply base coat; allow to dry thoroughly. Plan placement of grout lines; mark points of intersections on wall, using a pencil.

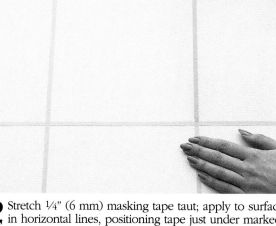

2 Stretch ¼" (6 mm) masking tape taut; apply to surface in horizontal lines, positioning tape just under marked points. Repeat for vertical lines, positioning tapes just to right of marks. Press tapes firmly in place with pads of fingers; do not burnish.

3 Apply desired faux finish. Allow to dry. Remove tapes.

4 Paint over the grout lines free-hand, using round artist's brush and desired glaze to contrast with faux finish. Allow lines to have some irregularity in thickness and density. Allow to dry. Apply finish or sealer to the entire surface as desired.

1 Follow step 1 opposite. Stretch ⅛" (3 mm) masking tape taut; apply to surface in horizontal lines, positioning tapes just under the marked points. Repeat for vertical lines, positioning tapes just to right of the marks.

2 Cut a triangle from horizontal tape, to the left of intersection with a vertical tape, using mat knife; angle-cut from upper point of intersection to lower left at 45°. Repeat for all horizontal tapes at each intersection.

3 Cut a triangle from vertical tape, just above intersection with a horizontal tape; angle-cut from left point of intersection to upper right at 45°. Repeat for all vertical tapes at each intersection.

4 Burnish all tapes, using a plastic credit card or similar tool. Apply faux finish. Allow to dry thoroughly.

5 Draw in shadow, ⅛" (3 mm) wide, above each horizontal tape, using marker in shade darker than the base-coat color; use ruler for accuracy.

6 Draw in shadow, ⅛" (3 mm) wide, to left of each vertical tape. Remove all tape from surface. Apply finish or sealer to the entire surface as desired.

Square tile effect is created by applying tapes at evenly spaced intervals, both horizontally and vertically.

Staggered stone block effect is created by first taping a grid for square tile effect and then removing alternate vertical sections.

Combined grout line patterns add interest to the faux finish.

Metallic
Finishes

ANTIQUED METALLIC FINISHES ON PAINTED SURFACES

Any surface that can be painted can be given an authentic antiqued metallic finish. Acrylic paints that contain finely ground metal particles, such as those developed by Modern Options, are painted onto a primed surface. Before the paint dries, Modern Options' antiquing solutions are applied; they react with the metal, causing verdigris patinas or rust to form. Copper Topper™, Gilded Gold™, Blackened Bronze Base™, and Blonde Bronze Base™ are acrylic metallic paints that can be antiqued with Patina Green™ and Patina Blue™ antiquing solutions, creating a verdigris finish. Silver Plate™ acrylic metallic paint can be given an antiqued look, using Burgundy Tint™ or Black Tint™ tinting solutions. Instant Iron™ acrylic metallic paint develops a rust when Instant Rust™ antiquing solution is applied.

Since the metal particles tend to sink to the bottom of the bottle, always shake the bottle well before, and several times during, application. Build up the paint base with several thin coats, allowing each to dry thoroughly before the next is applied. Apply antiquing solution to the top coat when it is still wet or tacky, allowing the solution to react with the metal. Once dry, a natural sealant in the paint prevents the solution from reacting with the metal particles, with the exception of Instant Iron, which can be antiqued while wet or dry.

Repeated applications of the antiquing solution will intensify the patina or rust finish. A matte aerosol acrylic sealer will prevent the finish from rubbing off when handled as well as prevent further natural aging of the piece.

Thoroughly read and follow the manufacturer's instructions for use of these products. Wear rubber gloves and goggles and avoid inhaling the fumes or vapors of the antiquing solutions.

HOW TO APPLY A METAL-LEAF FINISH

1 Apply thin coat of paint in the desired base-coat color over primed and sanded (page 18) surface, using sponge applicator; allow to dry. Repeat two or three times until painted surface is fully opaque.

2 Sand surface smooth, using 400-grit wet/dry sandpaper; wipe with damp cloth.

3 Apply light, even coat of size, using sponge applicator or brush; allow to set until clear, or about 30 minutes; surface will be tacky but not wet.

4 Cut the binding from book of metal leaf, using scissors. Remove two or three layers of metal leaf with supplied tissues at top and bottom; cut into quarters.

5 Hold piece of leaf between supplied tissues; avoid touching it directly with fingers. Slide bottom tissue from underneath leaf. Touching top tissue, press leaf in place over sized surface.

6 Remove top tissue. Using soft, dry paintbrush in an up-and-down motion, gently tamp the leaf in place to affix it. Then smooth leaf, using gentle stroking motion.

7 Apply additional pieces of leaf, overlapping them slightly, until entire area is covered.

9 Buff the entire surface gently, using soft cotton cloth. Apply two thin coats of clear finish or aerosol clear acrylic sealer to prevent marring and tarnishing.

8 Brush over the surface of leaf in circular strokes, removing skewings (page 24) of excess leaf at overlapped edges; reserve the skewings. Fill in any gaps by loading the brush with skewings and tamping in place. Reapply size to any gaps that will not hold skewings, using small brush. Allow to set; reapply skewings.

HOW TO MAKE A STENCIL FOR A METAL-LEAF DESIGN

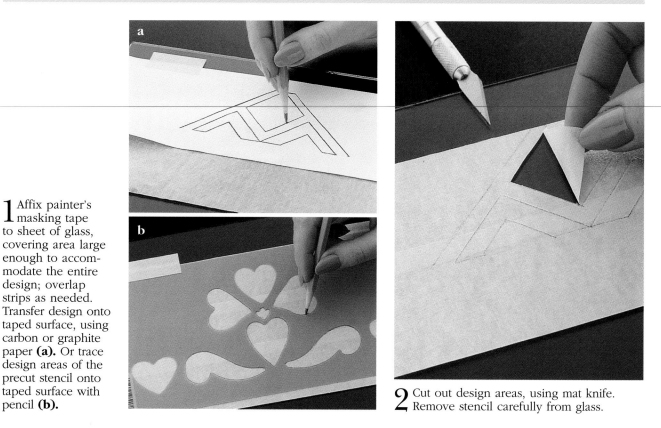

1 Affix painter's masking tape to sheet of glass, covering area large enough to accommodate the entire design; overlap strips as needed. Transfer design onto taped surface, using carbon or graphite paper **(a).** Or trace design areas of the precut stencil onto taped surface with pencil **(b).**

2 Cut out design areas, using mat knife. Remove stencil carefully from glass.

HOW TO APPLY METAL LEAF IN ISOLATED AREAS

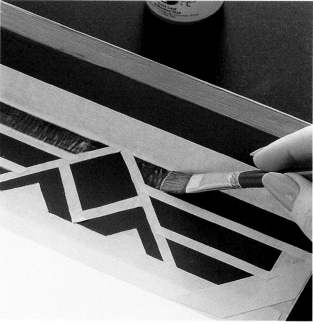

1 Prepare the surface, as in steps 1 and 2 on page 102. Mask off desired area, using painter's masking tape **(a),** or affix prepared stencil to surface **(b).** Press tape firmly in place, making sure all cut edges are secured.

2 Apply light, even coat of size to areas that will be leafed in first color, using small paintbrush; size may extend onto the tape, but avoid areas that will be leafed in a different color. Allow to set until clear, or about 30 minutes; surface will be tacky but not wet.

3 Apply leaf to sized areas, following steps 4 to 6 on page 102. Remove skewings and touch up gaps as in step 8 on page 103.

4 Repeat steps 2 and 3 for each additional metal-leaf color in design. Score metal leaf along edges of tape, using mat knife. Remove tape carefully. Apply clear finish or aerosol clear acrylic sealer to entire area.

HOW TO ANTIQUE A METAL-LEAFED SURFACE

1 **Pure copper or composition gold leaf.** Apply leaf as in steps 1 to 8 on page 102. Have a wet cloth near at hand. Apply antiquing solution to surface in fine mist, using spray bottle.

2 Watch carefully as the solution reacts with metal leaf. When desired effect is reached (this happens quickly), cover surface with wet cloth to neutralize solution; blot the entire surface gently to remove solution. Allow to dry completely. Apply two thin coats of aerosol clear acrylic sealer.

(Continued)

1 **Composition silver leaf.** Apply leaf as in steps 1 to 8 on page 102. Pour small amounts of tinting solutions into separate bowls. Dab solutions lightly onto surface, using desired applicators; blend solutions on surface to achieve desired effect. Allow to dry.

2 Speck (page 24) surface lightly, using black tinting solution and toothbrush. Allow to dry. Apply two thin coats of aerosol clear acrylic sealer.

MORE IDEAS FOR METAL-LEAF FINISHES

Speckled copper-leaf finish *(left and right) is achieved by applying adhesive size lightly to surface, using sea sponge. Leaf adheres in pattern left by sponge.*

Gold and silver skewings *(center) tamped randomly over a sized surface leave a free-form metallic pattern. Finely powdered skewings are dusted over the entire area.*

METALLIC COMPOSITE STENCILING

Wax-based metallic paints can be used to create intriguing stenciled designs. Using a technique called composite stenciling, simple individual stencils for each element in the design are repositioned repeatedly as the design is built up. For example, to stencil a bunch of grapes, the design may be built using two or three different circle stencils, varying in size, and two different leaves. Strategic placement and shading of the elements gives the design a three-dimensional appearance. Elements in the foreground are stenciled first, setting up the design lines. Background elements are partially stenciled and shaded to look as if they are behind the foreground elements.

Designs may be stenciled in a single metallic color or in multiple colors; the wax-based metallic paints are available in a wide variety of colors. A dark base-coat color provides the necessary contrast to the metallic paints for a dramatic effect. Select single stencils, such as leaves, flower petals, fruit, or berries. If desired, cut simple custom stencils, drawing inspiration from fabric, wallpaper, or design books. Practice the technique and test the design before applying it to the intended surface.

MATERIALS

- Low-luster latex enamel paint or craft acrylic paint in dark color for base coat; sponge applicator or paintbrush.
- Precut or custom stencils.
- Wax-based metallic paints.
- Stencil brush.
- Paper towels.
- Mineral spirits.

HOW TO STENCIL A METALLIC COMPOSITE DESIGN

1 Prepare the surface (page 18). Apply dark base coat; allow to dry. Position first stencil for element in central foreground of design.

2 Pick up small amount of wax-based metallic paint on stencil brush. Distribute paint to bristle ends, and remove excess by lightly rubbing brush in circular motion on paper towel, first in one direction, then in the other.

(Continued)

3 Hold stencil firmly in place with one hand. Holding brush perpendicular to surface and using circular motion, apply light layer of paint to open area; work around outer edges of stencil first.

4 Continue circular motion of brush, working toward center of stencil with gradually lighter pressure; allow color to fade away near center, creating shaded effect.

5 Reposition first stencil or position new stencil and repeat steps 2 to 4; repeat for all elements in foreground of design.

6 Position stencil for an element that appears in the background, overlapping foreground element. Apply the paint as in steps 2 to 4, fading away where the element disappears behind foreground element.

7 Repeat step 6 for all remaining elements of design, stenciling them in the order that they appear from foreground to background. Allow to dry. Apply several thin coats of aerosol high-gloss clear acrylic sealer, allowing surface to dry between coats.

8 Clean stencils by rubbing gently with paper towel dipped in mineral spirits. Clean brush by dipping in mineral spirits and lightly rubbing brush in circular motion on paper towel, first in one direction, then in the other.

MORE IDEAS FOR METALLIC COMPOSITE STENCILING

Repeating leaf designs are stenciled on the lid and sides of a decorative box.

Multicolor design accents a corner of a black picture frame.

Trompe l'Oeil
Effects

HAND-PAINTED TROMPE L'OEIL

Sophisticated trompe l'oeil murals have the ability to create visual space, almost to the extent that the viewer is tempted to walk into the scene. In some instances, paintings are so realistic that the viewer may attempt to reach for an object before realizing, in amazement, that it is merely a painted image. Such a level of sophistication, obtained by few artists, requires intense study and practice.

There are, however, some simple trompe l'oeil effects that can be successfully achieved with a less skillful hand. The success of the illusion depends on a few basic principals, including scale, perspective, and shading.

Begin any project by making a full-size drawing of the objects, including their shadows. Any alterations can then be made before transferring the drawing to the painting surface.

MATERIALS

- Drawing paper, pencil, ruler.
- Graphite paper.
- Craft acrylic paints in desired colors; white paint for mixing highlight colors; black paint for mixing shadow colors.
- Artist's brushes, such as a flat shader and a liner.

SCALE

Objects must be painted the size they would normally appear. Objects look smaller the farther away they are. If an image is to be viewed at close range, it should be painted life-size.

PERSPECTIVE

A sense of depth and distance can be developed by painting images in perspective. In a simple one-point perspective drawing, parallel horizontal lines that run from foreground to background seem to converge at a point on the horizon called the vanishing point.

SHADING

Determine an imaginary light source and add highlights and shadows to the painted images in reference to that light. For simple trompe l'oeil effects, paint each object in one color tone. Then add highlights by mixing white paint into that color. Paint shadows within the objects by mixing black paint into the original color. Shadows around objects should be painted by mixing black into the original color of the background. It is helpful to study still life photographs to determine the placement of highlights and shadows.

HOW TO DRAW AN IMAGE IN
ONE-POINT PERSPECTIVE

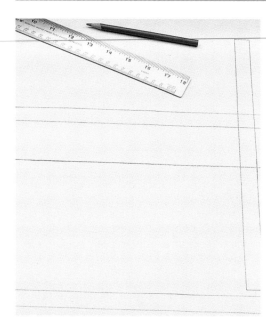

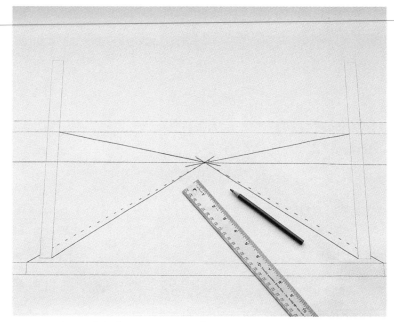

1 Draw a horizontal line (red) across the paper to represent the horizon, or eye level. Draw a point on the horizon to represent the vanishing point. Draw to scale primary vertical and horizontal lines (blue) in the foreground, placing horizontal lines a distance above or below the horizon equal to the actual distance they would appear above or below eye level.

2 Draw lines (blue) to represent all parallel horizontal lines that run from foreground to background, beginning each line in the foreground and converging all lines at the vanishing point. (Dotted lines show extension of converging parallel lines to vanishing point.)

3 Draw horizontal lines in the background, parallel to horizon line. Draw vertical lines in background. Draw any other connecting lines from foreground to background. Erase unnecessary lines to avoid confusion.

4 Add detail lines and round corners as desired. Erase any unnecessary lines.

HOW TO PAINT A
SIMPLE TROMPE L'OEIL IMAGE

1 Prepare surface (page 18). Apply base coat of the desired color. Allow to dry. Draw the image as in steps 1 to 4, opposite. Or, copy life-size images from magazines. Transfer the image to the surface, using graphite paper.

2 Paint image in single color tones, using desired artist's brushes. Allow to dry. Redraw detail lines.

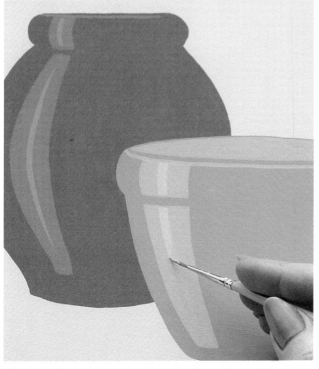

3 Mix lighter shades of each color, by adding white paint. Paint highlights in areas that would be in direct line with imaginary light source. Allow to dry.

4 Mix darker shades of each color, by adding black paint. Paint shadows that would be created if imaginary light source was shining on image.

TROMPE L'OEIL
STENCILING

For people who are less confident of their freehand painting skills, or would simply like to try another avenue, a trompe l'oeil effect can be created with stencils. There are some high-quality precut stencils available, with multiple overlays that help the artist create realistic, life-size images. With the use of shading and highlighting techniques, the artist is able to add depth and perspective, giving the stenciled images visual dimension.

Some of the more realistic stencils do not have the bridges, or blank spaces, so common with most stencils. Pinpoint registration marks ensure that each overlay lines up exactly over the preceding one. A pouncing (page 24) method of application, using craft acrylic paints, allows for successful blending of colors and shading. A wide selection of stencil brushes allows the artist to use a different brush for each paint color, in sizes proportionate to the sizes of the stencil openings. Masking tape wrapped around the bristles ¼" (6 mm) from the end helps support the bristles during the pouncing motion.

Follow the manufacturer's instructions and color suggestions for completing the stencil, or select color combinations as desired. Several colors may be applied with each overlay, depending on the complexity of the design. Each opening may receive a base color, applied in gradation shading, and then another color for darker shading in areas that would appear in shadow. As with other trompe l'oeil methods, determine an imaginary light source, highlighting foreground areas that would be in direct line with that light source and shading areas that would appear in shadow. After completing the stenciled image, add the shadow that the image would cast on the surface behind it.

MATERIALS

- Precut stencil with multiple overlays.
- Painter's masking tape.
- Craft acrylic paints.
- Stencil brushes.
- Disposable plates; paper towels.

HOW TO STENCIL A TROMPE L'OEIL IMAGE

1 Position the first overlay as desired; secure to the surface, using painter's masking tape. Mark the surface through registration holes, using sharp pencil.

2 Place 1 to 2 tsp. (5 to 10 mL) of paint on disposable plate. Apply masking tape around bristles, ¼" (6 mm) from the end. Dip tip of stencil brush into paint. Using circular motion, blot brush onto folded paper towel until bristles are almost dry.

3 Hold the brush perpendicular to the surface, and apply paint to the first opening, using up-and-down pouncing motion. Apply the paint lightly and evenly throughout the entire opening.

4 Deepen color to desired level by repeated pouncing in areas of the opening that would not be highlighted, shading darker into areas that would appear in shadow; leave highlighted areas pale.

5 Repeat steps 3 and 4 for all openings that receive the same color. Repeat step 2 with the shading color and another brush. Apply shading to areas of openings that would appear in shadow.

6 Repeat steps 2 to 5 for any additional colors on the first overlay. Remove overlay.

7 Position second overlay, aligning registration marks; tape to surface. Repeat steps 2 to 6 for second overlay. Repeat for any subsequent overlays until image is complete.

8 Follow step 2, opposite, using small stencil brush and gray or brown paint. Apply the paint lightly with a pouncing motion along the edges of image opposite light source, simulating shadows.

MORE IDEAS FOR TROMPE L'OEIL EFFECTS

Raised panels *are painted on an interior door, using precut stencils as a guide. Chair rail molding is an illusion created with trompe l'oeil stenciling.*

Mark placement for each panel on door. Move the stencil up or down to complete each panel. Follow the principle of shading (page 115) to determine dark and light areas.

Open window is painted in freehand trompe l'oeil, using one-point perspective (page 115). Stenciled flowers and greens suggest an outdoor flower bed.

(Continued)

MORE IDEAS FOR TROMPE L'OEIL EFFECTS
(CONTINUED)

Recessed nook *painted in freehand trompe l'oeil invites visitors to take a second look.*

Wood graining and stenciling *are combined to give a decorative box the illusion of carved wood.*

Prepare surface and apply wood-grain finish, stopping before final wash. Apply trompe l'oeil stencil over wood grain.

Complete wood-grain finish over stencil. Allow to dry. Apply satin clear finish.

INDEX

CY DECOSSE INCORPORATED
President/COO: Nino Tarantino
Executive V.P./Editor-in-Chief:
William B. Jones
Chairman Emeritus: Cy DeCosse

PAINTED ILLUSIONS
Created by: The Editors of
Cy DeCosse Incorporated

Group Executive Editor: Zoe A. Graul
Editorial Director: Dawn M. Anderson
Managing Editor: Elaine Johnson
Senior Project Manager: Kristen Olson
Associate Creative Director:
Lisa Rosenthal
Art Directors: Kathlynn Henthorne,
Mark Jacobson
Writer: Linda Neubauer
Editor: Janice Cauley
Researcher: Linda Neubauer
Sample Production Manager:
Carol Olson
Senior Technical Photo Stylist:
Bridget Haugh
Technical Photo Stylists: Sue Jorgensen,
Nancy Sundeen
Styling Director: Bobbette Destiche
Project Stylist: Coralie Sathre
Prop Stylist: Michele Joy
Lead Artisan: Phyllis Galbraith
Artisans: Arlene Dohrman,
Phyllis Galbraith, Valerie Hill,

Carol Pilot, Michelle Skudlarek,
Nancy Sundeen
Vice President of Photography &
Production: Jim Bindas
Director of Photography: Mike Parker
Studio Manager: Marcia Chambers
Lead Photographer: Charles Nields
Lead Assistant: Greg Wallace
Photographers: Bill Lindner,
Rebecca Schmitt
Contributing Photographer: Steve Smith
Print Production Manager: Patt Sizer
Senior Desktop Publishing Specialist:
Joe Fahey
Desktop Publishing Specialist:
Laurie Kristensen
Production Staff: Laura Hokkanen,
Tom Hoops, Jeanette Moss, Mike
Schauer, Mike Sipe, Brent Thomas,
Kay Wethern
Shop Supervisor: Phil Juntti
Scenic Carpenters: Troy Johnson,
Rob Johnstone, John Nadeau
Consultants: Paulette Johnson,
Elise Kinkead, Maureen Lyttle,
Katherine Joan Tilton
Contributors: Buck's Unpainted Furniture;
Deco Art; Designer Stencils®; Golden
Artist Colors, Inc.; Houston Art &
Frame; Jan Dressler Stencils; Modern
Options; Plaid Enterprises, Inc.;
Symphony Art, Inc.; Walnut Hollow

President/COO: Philip L. Penny

Also available from the publisher:
*Bedroom Decorating, Creative Window
Treatments, Decorating for Christmas,
Decorating the Living Room, Creative
Accessories for the Home, Decorating with
Silk & Dried Flowers, Kitchen & Bathroom
Ideas, Decorating the Kitchen, Decorative
Painting, Decorating Your Home for
Christmas, Decorating for Dining &
Entertaining, Decorating with Fabric &
Wallcovering, Decorating the Bathroom,
Decorating with Great Finds, Affordable
Decorating, Picture-Perfect Walls, More
Creative Window Treatments, Outdoor
Decor, The Gift of Christmas, Home
Accents in a Flash*

Printed on American paper by:
Quebecor Printing

99 98 97 96 / 5 4 3 2 1

Cy DeCosse Incorporated offers
a variety of how-to books. For
information write:
Cy DeCosse Subscriber Books
5900 Green Oak Drive
Minnetonka, MN 55343